IMAGES
of Rail

PLYMOUTH RAILROADS

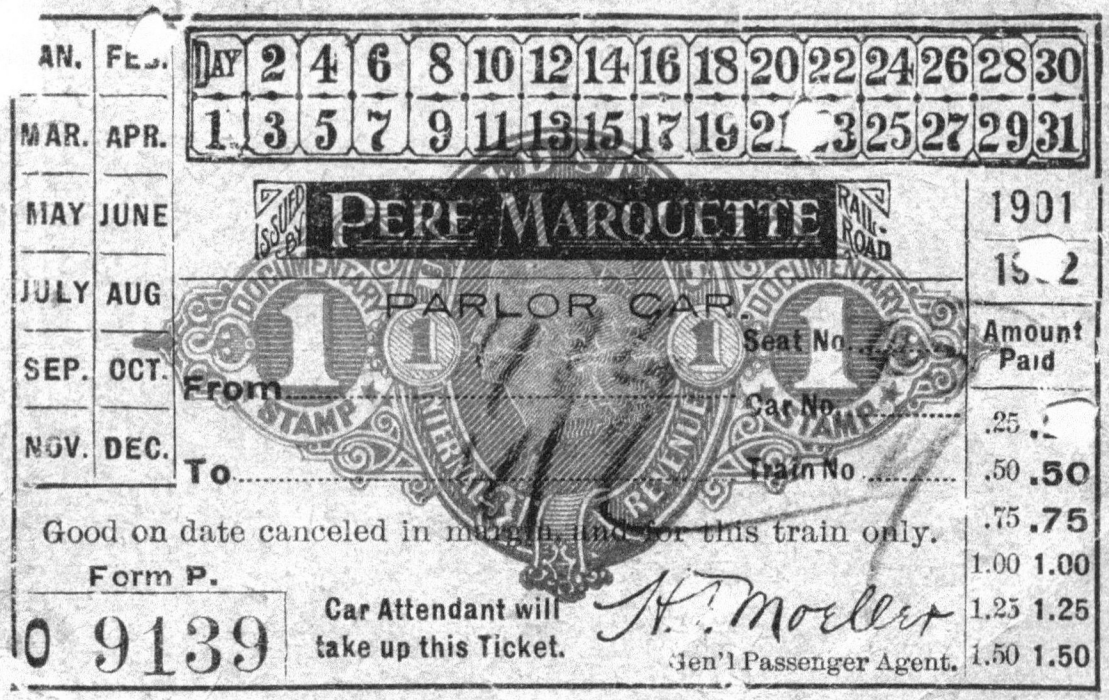

Here's your ticket to ride! Traveling on the Pere Marquette Railroad at the turn of the century was efficient, with tickets designed for easy customization. This parlor car ticket was used on February 23, 1902, for a fare of 25¢. The general passenger agent who issued it, H.F. Moeller, worked for the railroad for more than 10 years before leaving in March 1912. (Courtesy of the Plymouth Historical Museum.)

ON THE COVER: This photograph captures a moment in time as a steam engine arrives from Detroit at the Pere Marquette depot near the Starkweather Street crossing. In 1911, the restaurant and hotel east of the depot were open for business and offered respite for the weary traveler. This bustling stop also saw abundant freight traffic; note the cart piled high with packages awaiting transfers to their final destinations. (Courtesy of Clements Library.)

IMAGES
of Rail

PLYMOUTH RAILROADS

Elizabeth Kelley Kerstens and Ellen Elliott

ARCADIA
PUBLISHING

Copyright © 2020 by Elizabeth Kelley Kerstens and Ellen Elliott
ISBN 978-1-4671-0469-2

Published by Arcadia Publishing
Charleston, South Carolina

Library of Congress Control Number: 2019948888

For all general information, please contact Arcadia Publishing:
Telephone 843-853-2070
Fax 843-853-0044
E-mail sales@arcadiapublishing.com
For customer service and orders:
Toll-Free 1-888-313-2665

Visit us on the Internet at www.arcadiapublishing.com

Dedicated to our families, who lovingly supported us through this project: Coco, Zuzu, and Marty Kerstens and Joe, Jackson, and Melanie Elliott

Contents

Acknowledgments		6
Introduction		7
1.	Two Railroads Meet in a Burg Called Plymouth	9
2.	Streamlining into the Future	25
3.	Moving Air Rifles, Autos, and Sugar Beets	33
4.	Tragedy on the Rails	43
5.	Working on the Railroad	47
6.	Depots, Roundhouses, and the Plymouth Yard	53
7.	Hobos, Presidents, and Circuses, Oh My!	75
8.	Local Connections	87
9.	The End of the Train	105
Bibliography		126
About the Friends of the Plymouth Historical Museum		127

Acknowledgments

This book is all Chris Huffman's fault. As a Plymouth Historical Museum volunteer, he suggested a fundraising camp in anticipation of the arrival of a donated caboose from CSX. Liz had already written three Arcadia Publishing books and wasn't looking forward to the process of doing another. After weighing the pros and cons, she approached her friend Ellen to help alleviate some of the stress of researching and writing. Not knowing what she was getting into, Ellen said, "Sure!" Liz told Chris that the author application was submitted and quipped, "I'm not sure whether I should thank you or curse you for the suggestion." The reality has been far grander than either Ellen or Liz imagined.

Ellen and Liz are indebted to the following people and organizations for supplying photographs: Bob Bake; Bill Bresler; Gene Dickirson; Cynthia Hartsig; Peter Hayes; Dwight Jones; Ernie Krumm; Richard Laible; Jeff Mast; Mike Pappas; Chris Paciocco; Lynda Plotinski; Anthony Rzucidlo; Michael Shuster; Paul Snyder (Northville Historical Society); Mike Woloszyk; Archives of Michigan; Burton Historical Collection; Bentley Historical Library and Clements Library, both at the University of Michigan; Chesapeake & Ohio Historical Society; George A. Smathers Library of the University of Florida; Kalmbach Media; and Wayne Historical Museum.

Ellen and Liz are newly converted railroad geeks; this could not have happened without the knowledgeable assistance of some real railroad geeks. In addition to being the contractor for the caboose renovation, T.J. Gaffney quickly answered all of their questions and did an expert review of some chapters. Jonathon Leese was uniquely familiar with the Plymouth Historical Museum's caboose and the workings of the Wyoming Yard, greatly assisting with the caboose chapter. Brian Golden reviewed the interurban chapter. Joe Elliott reviewed text and provided inspiration and moral support. Marty Kerstens provided valuable assistance with the arrival of the caboose, being "voluntold" to create replacement doors that day and taking pictures when needed.

Special thanks to our "angels in the archive," Pam Yockey and Dan Packer, who enthusiastically dug through stacks and volumes of information and photographs at the Plymouth Historical Museum to find interesting tidbits for the book.

Unless otherwise noted, all images appear courtesy of the Plymouth Historical Museum.

INTRODUCTION

Before Michigan was a state, it had a railroad. The Detroit & Pontiac Railroad, the first such company in the Northwest Territory, was chartered in 1830. So began the tumultuous journey that attempted to link Michigan to the rest of the continent by rail. The succeeding years saw tremendous upheaval in the developing transportation infrastructure of the state. Lines were bought and sold and undercapitalized, went into bankruptcy, and experienced a variety of land-ownership issues that prompted numerous court cases, with some of them taking years to resolve.

In 1856, Congress passed legislation that allowed for land grants with certain stipulations. This encouraged the creation of rail construction to the northern lower peninsula of Michigan. The burgeoning lumber and mineral industries profited from this opportunity for virtually unlimited transportation of their goods.

The first railroad that would ultimately impact Plymouth was the Detroit & Howell Railroad, which was incorporated in 1864. The track was intended to run between Howell and Detroit, which would put Plymouth right in its path. The Civil War ended in 1865. As the nation healed, transportation and industrial growth blossomed. In an example of the volatility of the railroad industry at the time, before the tracks of the Detroit & Howell even reached Plymouth in 1871, the company was twice consolidated with other lines. One of the reasons for this instability was the collapse of an 1863 state-authorized bond issue program. This program allowed local municipalities to tax citizens, then those funds were handed over to the railroads. Once the state supreme court ruled the sale of these bonds as unconstitutional in 1870, all previously issued bonds became valueless.

In May 1871, the citizens of Plymouth held two separate celebrations. In early May, an excursion train of flatcars arrived on the new tracks between Wayne and Plymouth on the Holly, Wayne & Monroe Railroad. The train, loaded with Wayne dignitaries and the Wayne Cornet Band, was met at the Plymouth depot by the Plymouth Cornet Band and many local citizens, according to the May 4, 1871, *Detroit Advertiser and Tribune*. At the end of May, the first locomotive came into the village of Plymouth on the east–west tracks of the new Detroit, Lansing & Lake Michigan Railroad.

An article in the June 1, 1871, *Detroit Advertiser and Tribune* stated: "Few places in the state will have better railroad facilities than Plymouth when both roads are completed. With a rich farming country surrounding us, we flatter ourselves with the hope of a prosperous future. Real estate is held at reasonable prices, the day of speculative extravagances having passed."

Within a year, the entire ambiance of Plymouth had changed—it morphed from a sleepy, quiet, remote burg to a village filled with the chuffing, shrill, penetrating sounds of steam locomotives and the hustle and bustle of activities at the new depots.

"We had been sleeping for the last ten years," said a businessman in the March 14, 1872, *Detroit Free Press*, "but look all around. See that new brick building, these new houses, that surveyor in the meadow, those teams hauling lumber, those teams with goods, those cars filled with building material to be used here. In five years from now Plymouth will be one of the liveliest, busiest towns in Michigan. Families are moving in, houses are going up on every hand, merchants are increasing stock, manufacturers are looking around, and it's going to be a 'right smart' place."

Not only was the village of Plymouth prospering, but the people of Plymouth were also expanding their horizons. Excursions to Detroit via rail were common and cost 65¢ for a round-trip ticket, with activities that included watching the contemporary Detroit baseball team, picnicking on Belle Isle, and floating up the Detroit River into Lake St. Clair.

The growth of the railroads influenced Plymouth innovators to seize opportunities to create new industries and products. As in any capitalistic environment, some ventures thrived, and some withered on the vine. During the last two decades of the 19th century, the following companies prospered: Bennett & Son Fanning Mills, Markham Manufacturing, Plymouth Iron Windmill Company (later Daisy Manufacturing), Conner Hardware, Hall Washing Machine Manufacturer, Heide's Greenhouse, Hillmer Brothers, L.C. Hough Grain Elevator, Huston & Company Hardware, Lloyd Lewis Saw Mill, Andrew Lapham's General Store, Gayde's, William Wherry's Mole Trap, D.B. Wilcox & Son Flour Mill, and Shafer Brothers Foundry.

When the calendar turned to 1900, the Pere Marquette Railroad was born—a result of the consolidation of four Michigan-based railroads, including the two that ran through Plymouth. But the Pere Marquette was not without trials and tribulations. News about receiverships, restructuring, catastrophes affecting both infrastructure and people, and public perception dominated the headlines of the local papers.

According to the September 3, 1915, *Plymouth Mail*, "Officials of the Pere Marquette railway have been under the impression lately that the relations existing between them and the village of Plymouth have not been most cordial. Arrests of train crews for violating the village smoke ordinance and for the holding of freight trains on street crossings has not tended to assuage this feeling on the part of the railway officials."

With the advent of the automobile and the proximity of Plymouth to the rail lines, the first decades of the 20th century saw the emergence of component parts being shipped into and out of the area. As time went on, the growing national demand for automobiles made the Michigan rail lines essential.

Early in the morning of November 11, 1918, a piercing whistle sounded through the Plymouth Yard as the Pere Marquette roundhouse and locomotives in the yard celebrated the end of World War I. The end of another war spurred further growth within Plymouth industries and rail facilities.

In the November 27, 1931, *Plymouth Mail*, George Moffett of the Pere Marquette Railway stated: "One of the big advantages of Plymouth is its geographical location. Just near enough to Detroit to be easily accessible, yet far enough away to be free from many of the disadvantages of a large city. . . . Plymouth, as well as the territory between Plymouth and Detroit, is due for industrial growth within the next few years."

All of the turmoil in the rail industry in the 19th century was a trial run for the turbulence in the 20th century, as the Pere Marquette became part of the Chesapeake & Ohio Railway, which is now CSX Corporation.

During the nearly 150 years of railroads in Plymouth, the benefits have outweighed the temporary annoyances, as the railroad helped the area flourish by providing employment and growth opportunities that it otherwise might not have experienced. Plymouth owes its prosperity to the railroads.

One
Two Railroads Meet in a Burg Called Plymouth

Plymouth entered the railroad age in 1867, when land was cleared at Shearer's Cut to make bridges for the Detroit & Howell Railroad. By 1871, when the first railcars arrived in Plymouth, the line was known as the Detroit, Lansing & Lake Michigan (DL&LM) Railroad. During this tumultuous time, rail lines emerged and consolidated. The Holly, Wayne & Monroe Railway was incorporated in 1865; in 1872, it became part of the Flint & Pere Marquette (F&PM) Railway, which changed to F&PM Railroad eight years later. By 1876, the DL&LM had become the Detroit, Lansing & Northern, which was absorbed by the Detroit, Grand Rapids & Western in 1897. In 1900, the Pere Marquette (PM) Railroad emerged, and it ran in Plymouth for 47 years.

The Pere Marquette was constantly enhancing and upgrading its infrastructure and fleet. In 1911, it made necessary improvements to the Plymouth yard and other locations. Its fleet was increased by 12 first-class coaches, 2 combination baggage and mail cars, and 60 steam engines. The arrangement of the wheels on the steam engine was important. There were three different types of wheels: driving, leading, and trailing, with the latter two also referred to as carrying wheels, which were connected by axles and not powered or coupled. The number of carrying wheels of an engine, and their placement, had an effect on the weight distribution of the engine and was directly related to the expected performance. The driving wheels, connected by coupling rods, got their power from the locomotive's pistons and worked together to move the train. Locomotives were classified by wheel arrangement using the Whyte notation system, a three-number series separated by dashes. For instance, a Pere Marquette Mogul had a 2-6-0 wheel arrangement, indicating two leading wheels in the front of the engine, six driving wheels in the center, and zero trailing wheels behind the driving wheels.

Over time, the steam engine changed to accommodate the needs of the railroad to efficiently move passengers and freight. Sadly, by the late 1950s, demands for a more cost-effective and lower-maintenance engine rendered the steam locomotive obsolete and closed the chapter on the majestic steam era.

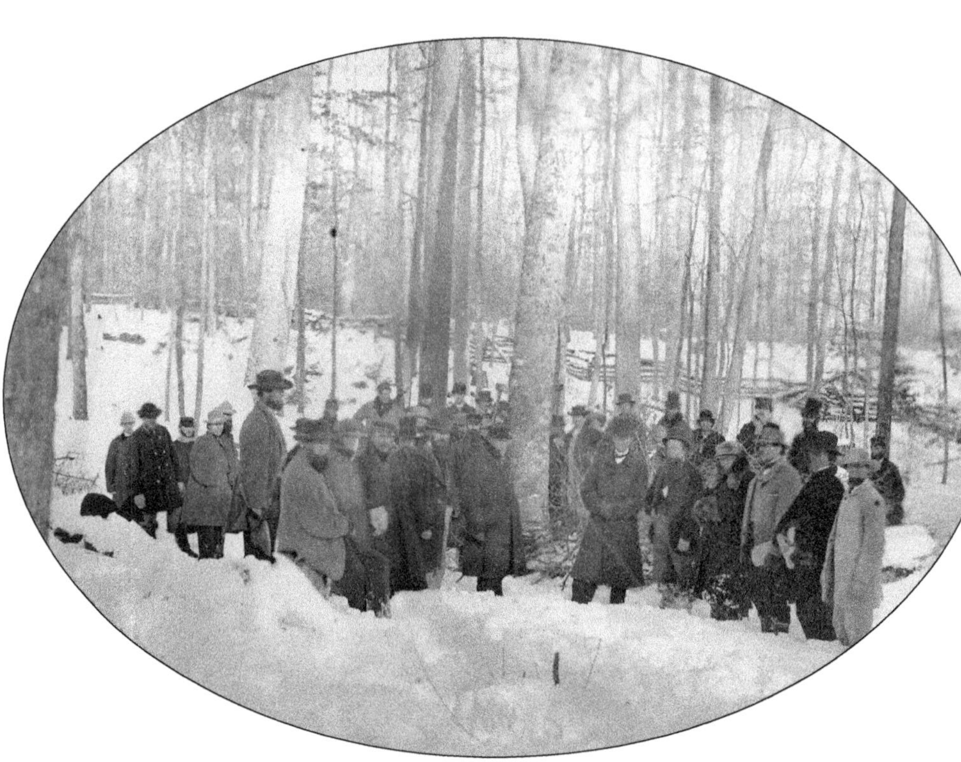

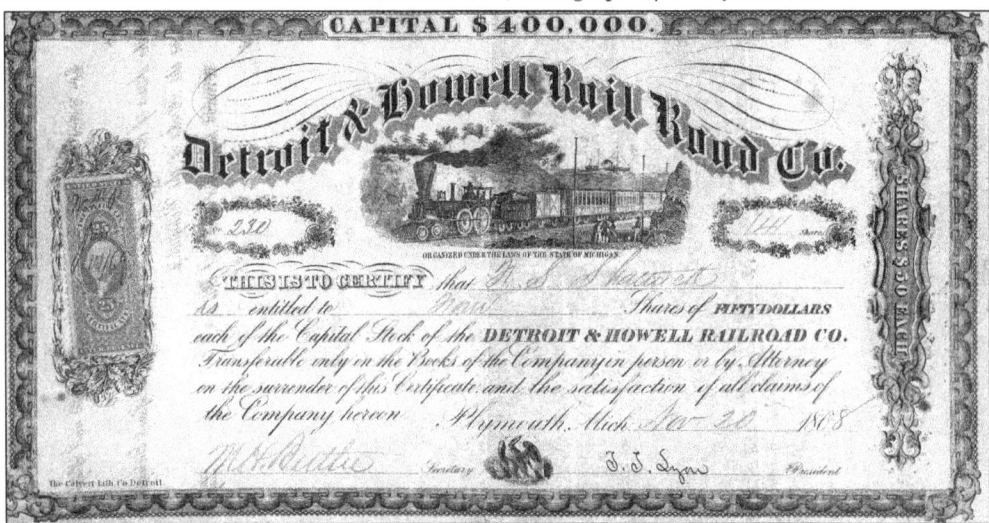

In February 1867, on wooded land owned by Jonathan Shearer just west of Plymouth, a tree-felling ceremony was held to inaugurate the construction of rail lines into Plymouth. Prominent citizens assembled to witness the ceremony, including George Starkweather and E.J. Penniman. The hardwood trees were cut by contractor S.A. Forbes of Detroit to make timber for the bridges and culverts for the Detroit & Howell Railroad. (Photograph by T.H. Johnson.)

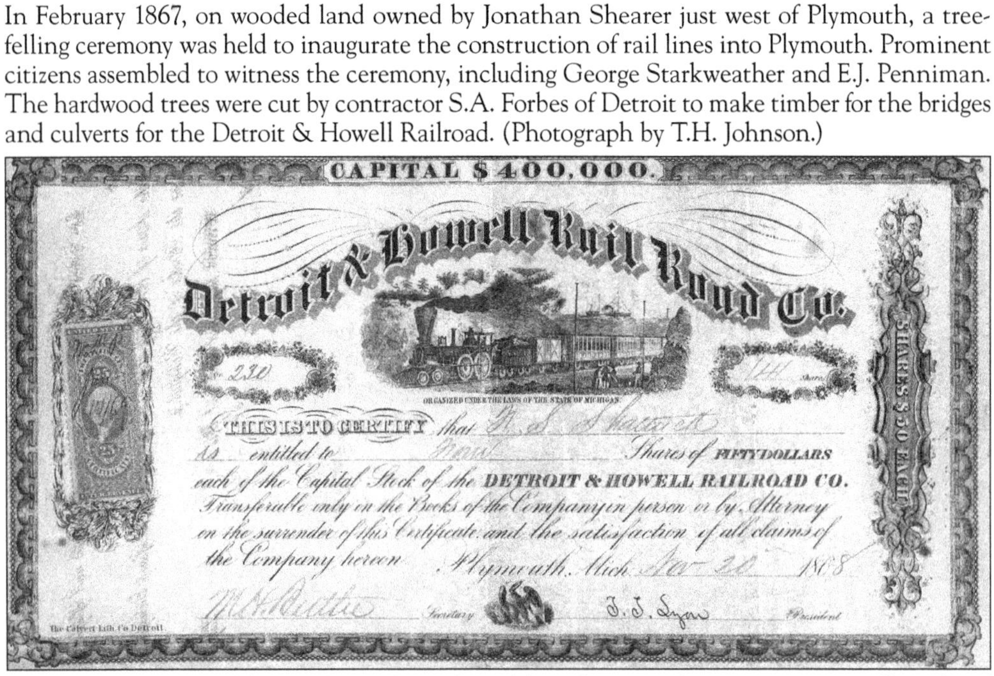

CAPITAL $400,000.

Detroit & Howell Rail Road Co.

230

4 shares

ORGANIZED UNDER THE LAWS OF THE STATE OF MICHIGAN.

THIS IS TO CERTIFY that F. S. Shattuck is entitled to Four Shares of FIFTY DOLLARS each of the Capital Stock of the DETROIT & HOWELL RAILROAD CO. Transferable only on the Books of the Company in person or by Attorney on the surrender of this Certificate and the satisfaction of all claims of the Company hereon. Plymouth, Mich. Nov 20 1868

Secretary

President

SHARES $50 EACH.

The Calvert Lith. Co Detroit.

Plymouth farmer Franklin S. Shattuck purchased four shares in the Detroit & Howell Railroad for $50 each on November 20, 1868. The railroad was incorporated in 1864 with planned capital stock of $400,000. By the time of the company's annual report in 1870, it had only received about $187,000 in capital stock. Although it had 52 miles of rail between Detroit and Howell, the road was unused.

This 1871 Michigan map drawn by Elam Jewett and Henry Chandler for the *Detroit Daily Post* shows the state of railroads at that time. Ownership of the lines during this tumultuous period was always a moving target. Some lines had difficulty capitalizing their stock, some had court challenges over land issues, and some went into receivership and frequently changed names. In 1871, the first year that trains came through Plymouth, the two lines were the Holly, Wayne & Monroe (north–south) and the Detroit, Lansing & Lake Michigan (east–west). Even then, however, the Holly, Wayne & Monroe was being operated by the Flint & Pere Marquette Railway, which absorbed the former railroad that year, according to the 1871 annual reports of both railroads. Also in 1871, the Detroit, Howell & Lansing Railroad consolidated with Ionia and Lansing companies to form the Detroit, Lansing & Lake Michigan Railroad Company, according to its annual report of 1871. The latter changed names two more times before consolidating with the Flint & Pere Marquette to become the Pere Marquette Railroad in 1900. (Courtesy of the Burton Historical Collection.)

Detroit, Lansing & Lake Michigan Railroad engine 18 had a 4-4-0 wheel arrangement; this type of engine was called the American. This type of engine proliferated on early railroads across the country because they excelled in the myriad road conditions they encountered, including steep grades, sharp curves, and uneven terrain. This engine, built around 1871 by Manchester, was scrapped before 1905. (Courtesy of Archives of Michigan.)

A flyer in the window of the John Steele and Roswell Root jewelry and drugstore on Plymouth's Main Street announces the change in schedule for the Detroit, Lansing & Lake Michigan Railroad's Detroit and Brighton trains beginning in July 1871. This store was adjacent to George Starkweather's general store and below Amity Hall, which was used for public meetings and entertainment. These buildings were destroyed by fire in 1893.

The Detroit, Lansing & Lake Michigan Railroad began carrying mail for the US government in 1872. For that service, the railroad received $1,025 per month. This car—being pulled by a 4-4-0 DL&LM engine—is adorned with lettering claiming its multiple functions. It reads: "United States Mail No. 77"; "Detroit, Lansing & Lake Michigan Baggage"; and "American Merchants Express Co." (Courtesy of Archives of Michigan.)

Detroit, Lansing & Northern engine 20 sits on a wooden bridge in Howell, Michigan, around 1893. This 4-4-0 American was built in 1873 by Manchester. It became engine 82 in the PM system, but its days were numbered by the time of the 1900 consolidation. Note the difference in the stack of this engine and the stack of the American shown on the previous page, which was built in 1871. (Courtesy of Archives of Michigan.)

In 1883, passenger service accounted for about a third of the earned revenues of the Detroit, Lansing & Northern (DLN) Railroad. In addition to facilitating local travel, the railroad successfully marketed trips to desirable destinations around the state, including Petosky, Traverse City, and Mackinac Island; Plymouth was one of the departure points on the line. *Detroit and the Pleasure Resorts of Northern Michigan*, a 94-page marketing brochure published by the DLN, contains a multitude of advertisements ranging from tourist hotels and spas to photographic establishments. That year, DLN carried 700,834 passengers, with an average distance of 24.44 miles traveled per passenger. Pullman sleeping cars were used during the summer months on trains running between Detroit and Mackinaw City. DLN paid the Pullman's Palace Car Company $906 in 1883 for the use of its cars, according to the company's annual report. Pullman cars could be found on about two-thirds of the railroad lines around the country at that time. The palace cars in which Pullman specialized were considered luxury railroad cars. (Courtesy of Library of Congress.)

The palace car Peggy, owned by the Flint & Pere Marquette Railway, was a unique combination of engine and passenger car. It was purchased in 1871 and had a wheel configuration of 4-2-4. It was used to ferry dignitaries and inspectors up and down the new rail lines built in the early 1870s. Peggy was F&PM's first palace car; the railway purchased two more in 1872.

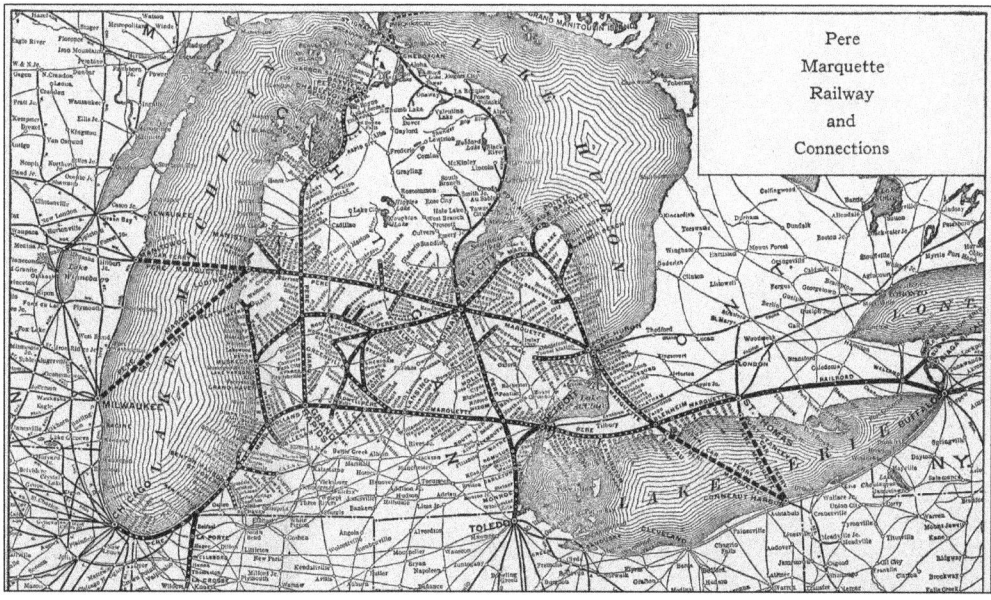

The Pere Marquette Railroad Company was incorporated in late 1899. It was a consolidation of the Flint & Pere Marquette Railroad; the Chicago & West Michigan Railroad; the Detroit, Grand Rapids & Western Railroad; and the Lowell & Hastings Railroad. This map shows the 1,650 miles of track that belonged to Pere Marquette on January 1, 1900. (Courtesy of Chesapeake & Ohio Historical Society.)

PM engine 84, with passenger cars in tow, waits by the depot around 1912. The facade of Dan Smith's remodeled restaurant and hotel is visible above the baggage car. This 4-4-0 engine was originally named City of Flint during its Flint & Pere Marquette Railroad days. F&PM rebuilt the engine in 1895; it was scrapped by PM in 1920.

In this photograph that looks west on Main Street in Plymouth, F&PM engine 87 is headed south and trailing a freight car from the Columbus, Hocking Valley & Toledo Railway. On the west side of the track, Bode's Hotel is just visible to the left, and the Plymouth Plank Road is visible in the foreground. Engine 87 had a wheel configuration of 2-6-0, was built in 1889 by Brooks, and was scrapped in 1927.

PM engine 235 is shown near the Starkweather Street crossing in front of Dan Smith's café prior to March 1908. Engineer Harry Laible, Smith's son-in-law, is sitting in the cab. Fireman Lee Passage is in the gangway. Standing from left to right are two unidentified people, George Knapp, Harry Coppernoll, and Ira Smith. This Mogul (2-6-0) was built in November 1888 by Brooks and scrapped in 1920.

The crew of PM engine 223 casually waits in the yard. Standing on the running board is fireman Harry Pelkey, with Milton Laible on the pilot beam. Standing on the ground are switchmen Ed Allen (left) and Robert Warner, with engineer Harry Laible in overalls on the right. Built by Brooks in 1898, this Mogul (2-6-0) was scrapped in 1937.

PM engines 225 and 227 sit on the tracks at the Plymouth Yard. These 2-6-0 Moguls were most popular on railroads that crossed flat terrain, like the Pere Marquette in Michigan. Built in 1898 by Brooks, they were scrapped in 1934. (Courtesy of Mike Pappas; photograph by Roy Hinkley.)

PM engine 393 pulls a passenger train on the north track heading east between Starkweather and Mill Streets in 1908. This Chautauqua type, later referred to as an Atlantic, was built in 1901 by Brooks with a 4-4-2 wheel arrangement. An increased heating surface and grate area—not possible with engines lacking trailing wheels—was achieved with a wide firebox located entirely behind the drivers and supported by the trailing wheels.

PM engine 394 speeds along the tracks across this trestle expanse over the Rouge River near Plymouth. The tenders for the 393 and 394 had capacities for 14 tons of coal and 4,500 gallons of water. Built by Brooks in 1901 with a 4-4-2 wheel arrangement, the 394 was scrapped after being in service for less than 30 years. (Courtesy of Mike Pappas.)

PM engine 720 appears here next to the concrete coal dock that was built in Plymouth between 1919 and 1920. This 4-6-2 Pacific was built by ALCO (Brooks) in 1921. After it was acquired by the Chesapeake & Ohio (C&O), the 720 was renumbered 419 but never repainted. It was retired in 1949 and sold to Luria Brothers for scrap the following year.

PM engine 1026 was built in 1918 by ALCO (Schenectady) as Wabash No. 2214 with wheel arrangement 2-8-2. According to the photographer, it is shown traveling northbound over the River Rouge east of Northville Road around 1943. It had a coal-tender capacity of 16 tons and carried 10,000 gallons of water. This was 1 of 55 Mikados owned by PM and was later reassigned C&O No. 2365.

PM engine 1199 was built by Baldwin in 1919 with a 2-10-2 wheel arrangement and was a Santa Fe type. It was purchased by PM from Hocking Valley and was originally numbered 143. Its tender could accommodate 18 tons of coal and 20,000 gallons of water. When the 1199 was acquired by the C&O, it was assigned number 2691 but was never repainted before being scrapped in 1949. (Courtesy of T.J. Gaffney.)

Art Norgrove stands in front of PM engine 1101, which was built in 1918 by ALCO (Dunkirk) with a 2-10-2 wheel arrangement. Its tender could carry 15 tons of coal and only 9,000 gallons of water—less than half of PM engine 1199's capacity. After being acquired by C&O, it was renumbered 2975. It was scrapped in 1952. (Courtesy of Lynda Plotinski.)

This shiny new PM engine 1216, with a wheel arrangement of 2-8-4, was known as a Berkshire. It was built in 1941 by Lima; note the manufacturer's label on the left. At the time, the 39 Berkshires owned by the railroad were the most powerful in its fleet. This engine was scrapped in May 1956. (Courtesy of Bob Bake; photograph by William S. Bake.)

In this October 1941 picture, PM engine 1211 chugs down the tracks with a manifest at Plymouth. No. 1211, a Berkshire built by Lima in 1937 as part of its first delivery of this class, was renumbered 2695 when it was transferred to C&O. (Courtesy of Chesapeake & Ohio Historical Society; photograph by Emery Gulash.)

Booster-equipped C&O engine 2695 charges ahead as it pulls a line of freight. One of the last steam engines in Plymouth, it was numbered 1211 when it was owned by Pere Marquette. It was scrapped in 1953. (Photograph by Romeo Wood.)

On this snowy day in February 1947, PM engine 1239 came into Plymouth from Toledo with a line of 65 cars. Built by Lima in 1944, and one of 39 high-performance engines belonging to Pere Marquette, this Berkshire was scrapped in 1961. (Courtesy of Chesapeake & Ohio Historical Society.)

Pictured here is C&O steam locomotive 305, a 4-6-4. Built by Baldwin in December 1941, this Hudson is one of eight made of the L2 class. The Hudson's arrangement, with fewer driving wheels compared to carrying wheels, made it well suited for traversing flat terrain at high speeds. All of the engines in this class were retired in the mid-1950s.

PM engine 402 had a wheel arrangement of 0-6-0 and was a switcher. Fireman Lawrence Hill is standing on the gangway at left. Engineer Harry Laible appears in the cab. On the right side of the image, Jack Stroll (left) is standing next to switchman Robert Warner as he relaxes at the front of the engine. The 402 was built in 1902 by ALCO (Brooks) and was scrapped in 1934.

The construction of the highway through the River Rouge park system necessitated the building of overpasses for the trains. Engine 1327 appears here in 1934 pulling a line of freight cars while a road is being constructed beneath the overpass. Built in 1923 by ALCO (Pittsburgh) with a 0-8-0 wheel arrangement, it was reassigned No. 357 when it became part of the C&O fleet. It was scrapped in 1950.

Two

Streamlining into the Future

While the Pere Marquette (PM) Railway was considered independent following the 1929 takeover by the Chesapeake & Ohio (C&O) Railway, management of the railroad was jointly conducted with C&O. Therefore, as the troubled decades of the 1930s and 1940s progressed, forward-thinking ideas were often tested on the PM rail lines within Michigan. The mix of flat terrain and steep inclines on Michigan's lines offered a variety of testing scenarios. Pere Marquette's switch to diesel-electric locomotives began in mid-1939, when the railroad purchased its first switcher of class DE-1. Five more diesel switchers had been received by March 1943, when production was halted by the War Production Board because of World War II.

The next incursion into diesel began when the PM introduced "America's First Postwar Streamliner," the Pere Marquette. The new postwar passenger service between Grand Rapids and Detroit used an E7 diesel locomotive pulling a standard configuration of seven cars, which included a railway post office baggage/express car, a full baggage car, four coach cars with lounge areas, and a dining car. The preinaugural eastbound run of the new service came through Plymouth on August 6, 1946, according to the August 9, 1946, edition of the *Plymouth Mail*. Regular service commenced on August 10 that year.

In June 1947, the PM Railway was merged into C&O; the former PM lines were called the Pere Marquette District. The Michigan freight lines were valuable to C&O primarily because of the cargo that was hauled in connection with the large automobile industry in the state. Additionally, the successful test of the streamliners in Michigan brought great hope for increased passenger service after the war. However, C&O's desire for the growth of passenger service had to compete with postwar cultural shifts. Air travel was becoming more popular and convenient, while family automobile travel skyrocketed as the interstate highway system expanded in the 1950s and 1960s. These transportation shifts ultimately contributed to the collapse of independent passenger services, leading to the creation of Amtrak in 1971.

Pere Marquette received its first diesel-electric locomotive in July 1939 from Electro-Motive Corporation, part of General Motors. It was a switcher designated as SW1 with engine number 10. It was painted black, as were the other five diesels that PM had received by 1943. Diesel switchers, mostly used around railroad yards, had higher cabs for greater visibility. This picture was taken in April 1940. (Courtesy of Ernie Krumm.)

C&O E8 engine 4018 is shown in 1960 heading east out of Plymouth carrying the Sportsman, a passenger train that ran between Michigan and East Coast cities. Note the "C&O for Progress" logo on the front of the locomotive. That campaign began in 1948 and was part of a much larger public relations effort after World War II. (Courtesy of Chesapeake & Ohio Historical Society; photograph by P.A. Shuster.)

Here, a freight train crossing Mill Street passes the old Plymouth depot. These DOT-111 tank cars were built in 1973 and designed to carry dangerous liquids, such as ethanol fuel. The cars have a maximum capacity of 34,500 gallons and have had numerous safety issues over the years. In 1865, crude oil became the first liquid to be carried by primitive wooden tank cars.

CSX GP9 engine 6028 and another similar engine pull a load of freight heading south on the tracks between Farmer and Main Streets in Plymouth sometime after 1980. Built in the late 1950s by General Motors' Electro-Motive Division, the GP9 was a four-axle road switcher diesel-electric locomotive. "Road switcher" means that the locomotive could handle switching and road work.

C&O C630 engine 2100 and C&O SD35 engine 7429 sit next to the Plymouth freight house's platform as they wait to assist westbound freight trains ascending the grade at Salem Hill. Engine 2100 was one of four C630s built by ALCO for C&O between 1965 and 1967 and was only used for about 10 years. (Courtesy of Chesapeake & Ohio Historical Society; photograph by Ron Piskor.)

This linen postcard advertises the new Pere Marquettes—passenger streamliners created with all-new components following the end of World War II. The trains were delivered in 1946, shortly before PM was absorbed into C&O. The dining cars were revolutionary in their table arrangements, as was the idea of providing hostesses. This experiment by C&O's chairman, Robert Young, was an ultimately unsuccessful attempt to avert the declining trend of passenger service.

Above, C&O coach 1701 is one of the cars picking up Plymouth passengers in 1970. PM 135 was built by Pullman-Standard in 1950 as a coach along with the Pere Marquettes. It sat 54, with additional lounge seating for 9. C&O renumbered it to 1701 and remodeled it as a food-bar coach. It later served as Amtrak coach 3925. Ridership on the passenger lines was down in 1970, which led to C&O running its passenger trains with only one coach. Below, C&O E8 engine 1472 unloads a passenger at the Plymouth depot on the east–west line. The dilapidated freight house is visible in the distance. (Both, courtesy of Chesapeake & Ohio Historical Society; above, photograph by Gene Huddleston.)

As passenger service waned in Michigan, C&O's Pere Marquette trains were reduced to carrying one coach. This 1971 photograph shows C&O E8 engine 1471 heading into Plymouth shortly before passenger service was completely shut down on the old PM lines. Amtrak took over passenger service in the United States on May 1, 1971. (Courtesy of Chesapeake & Ohio Historical Society; photograph by Gene Huddleston.)

CSX GP40-3W engine 9969 was built by EMD in 1967. While the engine appears to have two passenger cars attached, actually, it is CSX's geometry train, which reads the geometry of the tracks to collect data for maintenance purposes. This train stopped short of Main Street in 2015 so the crew could pick up a carry-out food order from Bode's Corned Beef House. (Courtesy of and photograph by Chris Paciocco.)

In these two images, the photographer caught a local engine and caboose moving a boxcar, then returning without it. Above, CSX GP38 engine 2174 pulls a boxcar and caboose in the Plymouth yard area. Engine 2174 has a Seaboard System paint scheme, dating the photograph to after 1982, when the Seaboard System Railroad became an operating company of CSX. Baltimore & Ohio (B&O) caboose 903897, pictured below, was built in 1980 by Fruit Growers Express and decorated with the Chessie paint scheme. This caboose, as well as the Plymouth Historical Museum's caboose, CO 904151, were part of the last order of Chessie cabooses in 1980. In an effort to reduce costs after deregulation, railroads started replacing cabooses with end-of-train devices in the 1980s. (Both, courtesy of and photograph by Anthony Rzucidlo.)

B&O GP38 engine 3816 and three other locomotives haul a line of freight cars past Bode's Restaurant at the Main Street crossing in Plymouth in June 1968. As early as 1875, Gottlieb Bode was the proprietor of City Hotel in the present-day location of Bode's. The restaurant was renamed Bode's Corned Beef House in 1979.

In this November 2011 photograph, CSX ES40DC engine 5275, trailing a long load of freight, sits idle. Meanwhile, CSX C40-DW engine 9047, loaded with coal, uses the passing siding track near Beck Road, where the coal train will begin its uphill climb over Salem Hill. (Courtesy of and photograph by Chris Paciocco.)

Three
MOVING AIR RIFLES, AUTOS, AND SUGAR BEETS

The advent of railroads in Plymouth provided opportunities for local businesses to broaden their exposure to customers across the country. Raw materials were brought in, and finished products were shipped out. The proximity of the railroad was vital to the success of companies like Daisy Manufacturing Company, which, in 1900, garnered $130,513 in sales of air rifles. The Alter Motor Car Company, in business from 1914 until 1917, was located adjacent to the Pere Marquette tracks on Farmer Street. In August 1915, the company was producing 40 automobiles per week and shipping to agents in seven states.

Industry in Plymouth saw tremendous growth as the 20th century progressed. In 1924, Burroughs Adding Machine Company purchased 142 acres of property on the east side of Plymouth with ready access to the railroad. On October 25, 1935, the *Plymouth Mail* reported that "Plymouth's smaller factories [were] busy as bee-hives." Companies like Dunn Steel, Plymouth Plating Works, Plymouth Tube, and Plymouth Felt Products prospered. Plymouth Screw Products, located on Amelia Street, made products for automotive, refrigeration, and electrical firms and produced 125,000 units a day. It shipped parts to Ohio, Indiana, and Pennsylvania. In 1946, Evans Products, headquartered on Eckles Road, manufactured bicycles, heating equipment, and plywood. In 1947, the company sold $23 million in products worldwide. It also developed different types of railroad loading equipment and railway cars that assisted in the safe and efficient transportation of raw materials and completed products.

The 1950s continued to see the rail system used by local companies like Daisy, Evans, Plymouth Felt, and Burroughs. In 1953, Pilgrim Drawn Steel, located on Mill Street, dispatched 300 railcars. Other companies shipping at that time included Wall Wire and the Bathey Company, which was filling three to five railcars per week with its torpedo nets. By 1965, Evans Products had spent $4.5 million to expand its railcar production facility to support a boom that would last for about 10 years. By 1976, Evans Products had closed its doors at the Plymouth location because of the decline in the railroad transportation business.

Above, C&O engine 766 sits on the railroad spur behind the Daisy Manufacturing plant in December 1949. The 2-8-0 engine, built in 1911 by ALCO, was number 617 for Pere Marquette. The engine and coal car were used as an auxiliary heat source while workmen changed Daisy's coal-fired boilers to use oil. The project was scheduled to be completed by the beginning of 1950. No. 766 was retired in February 1950 and sold for scrap. The aerial photograph of Plymouth at left was taken in 1938. It captures the Markham/King plant (upper left) east of the tracks and Daisy Manufacturing Company (center right) west of the tracks. At that time, Daisy owned King Air Rifles but was no longer using the building for manufacturing. Access to the tracks was vital to the success of Daisy. (Above, photograph by John Gaffield; left, photograph by Cass Hough.)

Williams Brothers was established in Detroit in 1881 and incorporated in 1901. In 1908, the company purchased property from George Peterhans and built a tomato-canning factory east of York Street at the Pere Marquette tracks in Plymouth. The company had its own railroad siding, as it turned out 3,500 barrels of tomato pulp in 1908, which equated to 35 carloads with 100 barrels to each car. (Photograph by Davis Hillmer.)

The Bennett farm, located on the corner of today's Ann Arbor and Sheldon Roads, grew the popular crop sugar beets. Along with other local farmers, the Bennett family shipped their haul by rail to Saginaw, where multiple factories created sugar. Sewell (far right in the train car) and Paul Bennett (holding the flag) help unload at the railyard. Nearly 79,000 acres of sugar beets were grown in Michigan in 1913.

Plymouth Creamery Company was incorporated in June 1902. It was located just north of the J.D. McLaren Company, allowing it to use the Pere Marquette siding to distribute its popular butter. In 1907, farmers from Plymouth and surrounding communities brought in 28,000 pounds of milk per day, while the creamery churned out four tons of butter per week, according to the Plymouth Mail. (Photograph by Charles Draper.)

By 1903, ownership of the Plymouth Cheese Factory, located west of the depot on Starkweather Street, had been transferred to Fred Warner, pictured here in 1908. In addition to serving as governor of the state of Michigan, he was the successful owner of 13 cheese factories. Warner Cheese was shipped all across the country. (Courtesy of Library of Congress.)

In November 1901, J.D. McLaren & Company purchased the L.C. Hough & Son elevator business, situated on Main Street just east of the Pere Marquette tracks. McLaren dealt in hay and produce and had elevators in Salem, South Lyon, and Novi, according to the November 1, 1901, *Plymouth Mail*. McLaren received, sold, and shipped produce and other commodities and operated the elevator for PM. J.D. McLaren died in 1915; his company was sold in 1917 and became the Plymouth Elevator Company (above). In 1923, Plymouth Elevator advertised rail carloads of seeds and fertilizer; in 1938, the company advertised roofing materials and siding arriving by railcar. At some point, the McLaren family regained ownership and renamed the company McLaren Lumber & Coal. The company closed in 1975. (Above, courtesy of Cynthia McLaren Hartsig.)

Evans Products moved to Plymouth in October 1945. The company occupied the former Kelsey-Hayes plant on Eckles Road, where machine guns were manufactured for the war effort. This conversion was an important aspect of building the peacetime economy. The location—near the Pere Marquette Railroad—was essential for shipping products. The Evans Auto Loader was made here and is said to have saved the railroad, automobile companies, and receivers $500 million after its introduction in 1932. The above photograph shows models of the company's new six-car auto loader and the Evans D-F loader, which was designed to lock in freight and transport it "damage-free" to its destination. The 1965 photograph below depicts one half of a new special car that could carry 100 tons of steel coils—twice the amount that previous models could accommodate.

The Alter Motor Car Company was located west of the railroad tracks near Farmer Street. The company produced two models: a five-passenger touring car, shown here, and a roadster. In August 1914, the company shipped a carload of automobiles to Des Moines for display at the Iowa State Fair. Within three years, Alter Motor Car was out of business; the factory was sold to the Detroit Seat and Tank Company.

The Plymouth Motor Castings Company supplied parts for the automotive industry. In August 1916, a stock offering was announced as the business was expanding. The stock certificate shown here was for the purchase of 20 shares by local businessman W.T. Connor on April 24, 1917. By November 1918, the plant had been sold, as the location on Goldsmith was valuable because of its proximity to the railroad tracks.

D.B. Wilcox & Son took over Henry Holbrook's Plymouth Mills in 1879. After David (D.B.) died in 1902, the company became known as Wilcox Brothers Mills. The above photograph was taken from the nearby railroad bridge in 1911. Proximity to the railroad helped the Wilcox family receive carloads of poultry feed, and they offered free delivery in Plymouth. They also made and sold Fancy Blend Plymouth flour. Phoenix Mill, on the far side of the Phoenix Bridge in the photograph at left, was built in the 1840s. At the end of the 19th century, the mill changed hands numerous times and was constantly threatened by the millpond dam bursting. Last owned by the Plymouth Food Company, which briefly produced Plymouth Wheat Flakes, the mill burned down in July 1905. (Above, photograph by Davis Hillmer; left, photograph by Charles Draper.)

The October 24, 1924, edition of the *Plymouth Mail* announced that Burroughs Adding Machine Company had purchased 142 acres of land on Plymouth Road near the Pere Marquette Railroad. By 1938, this building was completed and occupied. The railroad spur coming into the plant from the north is visible in this photograph. By 1942, production of portable adding machines was restricted to filling the needs of the Army and Navy.

Located on the corner of Mill and Amelia Streets, the Bathey Manufacturing Company moved from Detroit in 1948 to occupy the former site of Standard Products Company. The company manufactured stampings and machine parts and initially employed about 100 men. In September 1956, a contract was awarded to Bathey for the production of parachute packs for the Navy, according to the *Detroit Times*.

On July 25, 1924, the *Plymouth Mail* reported that Dunn Steel was "nicely under production" in Plymouth. The above photograph shows its original location at 377 Amelia Street, just east of the railroad tracks. In 1935, it was running two shifts and produced clevis pins, bolts, and other parts for the automotive industry. The company went on to produce ball studs, which are an integral part of automobile suspension systems. In the 1950s, Dunn Steel became part of the Townsend Company, and production grew rapidly. In 1953, property for a new plant was purchased west of Starkweather Street on Dunn Street north of the old plant. In 1975, the company occupied 60,000 square feet on that site, as shown below, and received an order for tool shanks for use on machines digging trenches for the pipeline in Alaska.

Four

Tragedy on the Rails

Safety on the rails has been a concern since the first locomotive rolled into town. While measures were constantly introduced to help avoid disasters, unfortunate events still occurred. Crashes between trains were often a result of human error after a misread order or a switching mistake. One such incident occurred in September 1909, when two freight trains crashed, resulting in an engine being thrown from the track, several cars being crushed, and a load of peaches going up in flames. Miraculously, there was no loss of life.

Catastrophic train wrecks occurred on the Pere Marquette rails in this area in 1901 and 1907, with the latter referred to as one of the worst railroad disasters in the state of Michigan. In September 1913, Gasper Carbullo was working in the Pere Marquette yard when his coworkers made every attempt to alert him to an approaching 20-car freight train. He failed to react in time and was run over by the train, suffering fatal injuries. A similar incident occurred in August 1916, when Fred Williams was walking too close to the tracks as a westbound Pere Marquette passenger train advanced. He misjudged the distance and was struck by the engine and later died. Yardmaster Frank Losee also lost his life on the job in 1920, when he was hit by a section speeder.

By 1931, the Pere Marquette Railroad reported that "the greatest danger confronted by railroads is the hazard imposed upon them by automobile drivers. Practically all of the train wrecks of the past two or three years have been due to automobiles driven in front of trains or autos that were stalled on the tracks."

Train derailments were common as well, although these did not cause loss of life—just mere inconvenience. In August 1975, an 80-car train derailed just east of Sheldon Road. It was carrying a load of corn syrup, which created a sticky mess to clean up. Three other trains derailed that year, the causes of which were undetermined. Technological improvements have helped to significantly reduce the number of railroad disasters.

On Saturday, July 20, 1907, an eastbound Pere Marquette passenger train collided head-on with a westbound six-car freight train at Van Sickle Cut, a few miles west of Plymouth. Because of the steep curve in the terrain, neither engineer could see the other train until it was too late to stop. More than 30 people died, and more than 100 were injured in the accident. Plymouth doctors A.E. Patterson and Robert Cooper, along with physicians from surrounding areas, responded to the wreck. As shown in the above photograph, many people were curious and came out to view this tragedy. The mangled carnage of car 290 is shown in the photograph below. (Both, photograph by Lyman L. Ball.)

The above photograph shows car 290 from another angle. The below image shows a barely discernable boiler in the wreckage. An inquiry determined that the accident was caused by carelessness on the part of freight train conductor Fred Hamilton, operator W.A. Cassady, and train dispatcher Marcus Bonsell. Orders were misread, and the freight crew thought it had more time before the passenger train was expected to pass, which turned out to be a deadly assumption. The cleanup from this catastrophe caused great mental anguish, as the passengers involved were Pere Marquette employees and their families on an excursion from Ionia. It is said to be one of the worst train disasters in the history of the state of Michigan. Word of this incident spread across the nation; reports appeared in newspapers as far away as Los Angeles. (Above, photograph by Charles Draper.)

A horrific crash between a freight train and a passenger train occurred near the Plymouth yard on January 12, 1901. The express car of the latter telescoped into the locomotive's tender, fatally wounding engineer Elliott Moore and fireman John Kennedy. William Blische, engineer of the freight, also died. This photograph shows the nearly unrecognizable engines that were involved in this head-on collision. (Courtesy of Chesapeake & Ohio Historical Society.)

August 19, 1913, was another tragic day on the Pere Marquette. The accident pictured here was caused when some freight cars were separated from their engine and crashed into a switch engine in the yard. Engineer George Kramer and Lawrence Hill narrowly escaped death. By the next day, a wrecker was on the site to begin the cleanup. (Courtesy of Clements Library.)

Five

WORKING ON THE RAILROAD

The railroad required many people serving in varied capacities to sustain an efficient system. Executives, accountants, real estate agents, secretaries, and office workers managed one side of the business, while skilled tradesmen like boilermakers and blacksmiths were staples in the yard to assist in maintaining equipment. Engineers and conductors ensured that the trains ran on time, while freight agents and ticket agents managed the cargo and passengers. Inspectors played an important role in ensuring that the tracks, trains, and other infrastructure were in good working order to increase the opportunity for a safe work environment. Gandy dancers were integral to replacing track when needed and laying new track. Physicians were necessary to attend to workers' needs on a daily basis; they were also the key to saving lives when disaster struck. In Plymouth, Dr. A.E. Patterson was one of the Pere Marquette doctors who saw devastation of historic proportions during the massive wreck of 1907 and did his best to alleviate the pain of those who survived.

Advancements in technology and decline in passenger service contributed to the reduction in the necessary workforce. This was evident in 1953, when Archie Meddaugh, a brakeman and yard switchman for the Pere Marquette and later for the Chesapeake & Ohio Railway, retired after 42 years of service. Meddaugh was responsible for switching points that covered a 10-mile area and was well known for riding his bike on the job after selling his car to a war plant employee in 1941. In 1952, his position became obsolete with the installation of electronically controlled switches at the freight yards, which allowed switches to be automatically opened and closed from a central control panel. Like so many others, Meddaugh was employed by the railroad for his entire career and enjoyed his job. When his retirement was announced in the *Plymouth Mail*, he said, "my years with the railroad have been pleasant ones."

Even though the workforce has seen a reduction in numbers over the years, railroad workers have remained faithful to this iconic institution.

The yard workers shown here in front of the Plymouth roundhouse in 1937 were tradesmen, including blacksmiths and boilermakers. Another necessary job was that of the hostler, who moved engines in and out of the roundhouse. Wipers also worked here and were tasked with greasing the internal moving parts of the engines; note some of the particularly grimy-looking fellows in this lineup.

Trackmen, or gandy dancers, lay track in the Pere Marquette yard in Plymouth near where the track turns west of Starkweather Street. "Gandy dancer" was a slang term used to describe section hands who laid and maintained railroad tracks in the years before machines took over. (Photograph by Davis Hillmer.)

Freight agent George Carlson is seated inside an office of the Pere Marquette Railroad. He was responsible for all aspects of shipping goods to and from the station and ensured that loads were properly packed and documented. A bill of lading was a receipt given to the shipper. A waybill, detailing the shipment instructions, was also issued and accompanied the cargo on the way to its destination. (Courtesy of Clements Library.)

William S. Bake was a civil engineer for the railroad in the early 1900s. As lines expanded to northern Michigan, he used topographical studies to decide where the rails should run. He eventually became the general real estate agent for the Pere Marquette and would ride the train every day to his office in Detroit. He is pictured here at his home on Penniman Avenue. (Courtesy of Bob Bake.)

Art Norgrove moved to Plymouth around 1913 from Au Sable, Michigan. He is pictured here at work in the cab of an engine in the Plymouth yard. He was employed by the Pere Marquette Railroad and eventually retired from his job as a switch engineer with the C&O Railway. He died on February 27, 1961. (Courtesy of Lynda Plotinski.)

Railroad inspectors had an important role in helping to prevent train disasters. Examination of the tracks was a priority, and expediting repair orders was integral to the health of the system. Inspectors used specially equipped cars to assist them with their tasks. This 1956 Pontiac Chieftain, modified to ride the rails, is pictured on the track near the Starkweather crossing.

This 1921 physical examination record for Ernest Krumm certifies that he had 20/20 vision, was not color-blind, and had sufficient hearing capability. Passing these tests was necessary for all railroad employees in order to ensure a safe work environment. Krumm worked as both a hostler and a coal dock operator for the Plymouth railroad until his retirement. He died in 1969 and is buried at Riverside Cemetery. (Courtesy of Ernie Krumm.)

Engineer John Miller (left) and fireman G. Bousquette are shown on a Plymouth switcher job at Green Oak in October 1944. This PM engine 1109 is a 2-10-2 Santa Fe built by ALCO (Dunkirk) in 1918. It was later renumbered 2983 when it went into service with C&O. It was scrapped in 1950. (Courtesy of Ernie Krumm.)

Engineer John Miller appears in this photograph with his wife, Beulah, on the footboard of engine 84. John was an engineer living in Freeport, Michigan, in 1920. By 1927, he was in Plymouth working for the Pere Marquette Railroad, which became part of C&O Railway in 1947. He died on November 8, 1965. (Photograph by Bob Gray.)

In December 1898, Charles Draper was traveling on a freight to Detroit via Wayne. When he assumed the freight would stop and it didn't, he decided to jump. The *Plymouth Mail* reported "he not only did not plow up the ground with his face for several rods, but he did not even disarrange the creases in his pantaloons." This photograph is a reenactment of that event. (Photograph by Charles Draper.)

Six
DEPOTS, ROUNDHOUSES, AND THE PLYMOUTH YARD

George Starkweather was one of the influencers who brought railroads to the village of Plymouth. As work on the tracks for the Detroit & Howell Railroad progressed, Starkweather leveraged his authority when decisions were made regarding where the trains would stop. On July 22, 1868, he sold 3.1 acres of land for $285 to the Detroit & Howell Railroad for a proposed depot in the north end of the village. This same spot has housed a depot ever since, but today, it is used for commercial purposes.

On September 18, 1871, Siron Kellogg of Plymouth gave a small parcel of his land in trust (and for $1) to the Holly, Wayne & Monroe Railway for the sole purpose of building a depot for that north–south line. This depot was used until the late 1890s and was moved in 1903. In early May 1871, Plymouth held a celebration when the tracks of the Holly, Wayne & Monroe Railway reached the village. Citizens continued to celebrate when the first locomotive on the east–west line reached Plymouth at the end of that month.

While railroad ownership throughout Michigan was in turmoil in the last quarter of the 19th century, Plymouth was coming into its own as a major junction for trains headed to Grand Rapids, Lansing, Detroit, Flint, Monroe, and other destinations. Because of this, the Plymouth yard grew in importance in terms of engine maintenance, freight and passenger service, and advancing railroad technology. A two-stall roundhouse for engine repairs was added in 1892; by 1921, the roundhouse had been moved and had increased to 15 stalls.

Passenger service was offered on both lines from the beginning, with changes in the service occurring during the World Wars and the Great Depression. Passenger service declined as other modes of transportation became more popular. On May 1, 1971, passenger service was discontinued in Plymouth and elsewhere in Michigan as Amtrak took over and consolidated passenger lines. The demise of passenger travel in Plymouth also signaled the demise of nearby hotels that had catered to the traveling public for many years.

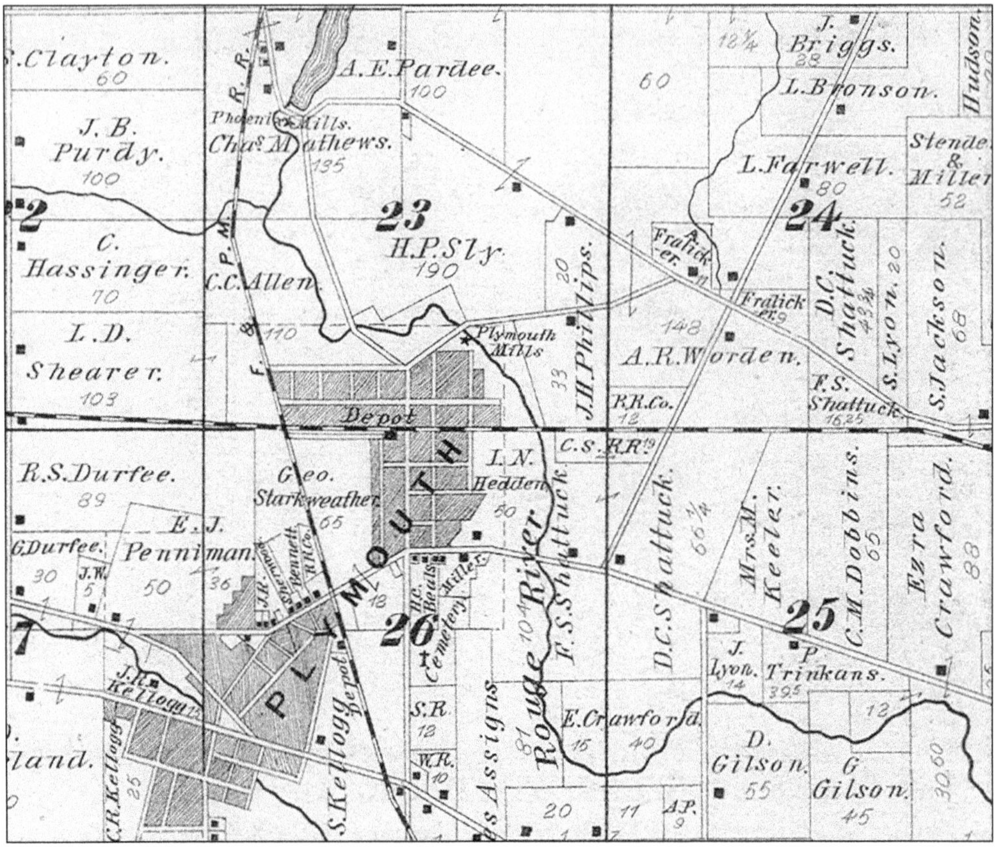

The above close-up of the Plymouth village area—from the Plymouth township map in the 1876 *Illustrated Historical Atlas of the County of Wayne, Michigan*—pinpoints the location of each of the Plymouth depots on the railroad lines. At that point, the north–south line belonged to the Flint & Pere Marquette Railway, and the east–west line belonged to the Detroit, Lansing & Northern Railroad. While both lines had depots from the early 1870s, after a fire destroyed the station on the east–west line in 1893, the original depot on the north–south line (below) served both lines until a new station could be built. This depot was reported closed in a May 1900 *Plymouth Mail*. The same newspaper reported in August 1903 that John McLaren had purchased the depot and was moving it to his elevator site for storage.

The depot belonging to the Flint & Pere Marquette Railroad (north–south line) is shown at the bottom of the 1893 Sanborn Fire Insurance map below. As noted, the passenger depot was in the north third of the building, and the freight house was in the remainder. Near the top is the L.C. Hoff (Hough) & Son Grain Elevator, situated adjacent to the tracks. This business was purchased in 1901 by McLaren & Company. By 1909, the Sanborn Fire Insurance map at right shows that the depot was gone from its 1893 location, while the J.D. McLaren Company had gained a hay and produce warehouse the same size as the former depot. On the former depot property, the village of Plymouth built a municipal electric light plant. (Both, courtesy of Environmental Data Resources.)

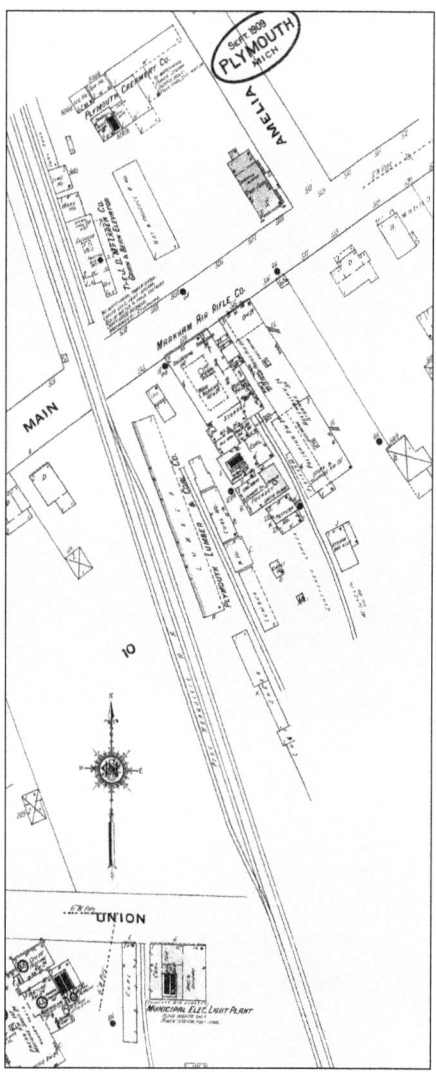

A lightning strike and fire on July 7, 1893, burned down the original depot and freight house (built before 1875) on the east–west Detroit, Lansing & Northern line. Both were rebuilt later in 1893. By 1900, when this photograph was taken, the east–west line was part of the newly formed Pere Marquette Railroad.

In March 1908, Dan Smith's family awoke to what they thought was an earthquake. Their home was on the second floor of this building, which housed the Pere Marquette Café. However, it was not an earthquake that startled them but rather a caboose slamming into the building. This mishap was the result of a switching error that allowed a train to travel unexpectedly from the yard and derail. (Photograph by Charles Draper.)

The train that struck Dan Smith's café caused tremendous damage to the building, which began as a seven-by-nine-foot lunchroom in the 1890s and was expanded over the years. The veranda that was added in 1899 was severely compromised and needed to be held up by supports. It wasn't until April 1909, more than a year after the accident, that Smith received payment from the Pere Marquette Railroad for the damage.

Located on North Mill Street, the Commercial Hotel (or Hotel Victor) appears on the 1893 Sanborn map (partially shown on page 55). When temperance leader Carry Nation came to town in 1908, she needed a place to stay. Karl Starkweather wrote in a memoir: "'Do they sell liquor there?' she asked. Someone said, 'Yes they do.' Nation then yelled out, 'So you have hell holes in this town. Well, I wouldn't sleep in a hell hole for love or money!'"

After reaching a settlement with the railroad, Dan Smith began rebuilding his restaurant in late April 1909. He wisely decided to move it about 10 feet back from the track. By June, the construction of a new facade, wraparound porch, and installation of plate-glass windows were almost finished. This structure survived well into the 1920s as a popular place for travelers to gather and enjoy a meal.

The Plymouth depot was bustling with both passenger and freight service after the start of the 20th century. This photograph was taken some time after June 1909 but before October 1910, as Dan Smith's new porch is visible on the left, and the hotel next to the depot has yet to be constructed. The Hotel Victor, located on Mill Street, is visible just beyond the steam engine. (Courtesy of Clements Library.)

As railroad business thrived, the need for improved infrastructure was evident. Travelers wanted accommodations that were convenient and comfortable. Construction of the hotel to the east of the depot began in October 1910. In January 1911, it was open to the public and could accommodate 22 guests. By February of that year, proprietor Frank Pierce was doing well, with the restaurant and hotel bringing in $1,000 combined for that month.

This photograph, taken after 1911, shows a flurry of activity at the Plymouth depot with passenger trains on both tracks. Dan Smith's café is completed on the left side of the tracks. To the right of the tracks, next to the hotel, the US Express Company had a small building east of the depot for use as a storeroom and office. (Courtesy of Clements Library; photograph by Davis Hillmer.)

This image of the Pere Marquette depot was taken between 1910, when Roderick Cassady became cashier for the depot, and 1915, when he moved on to manage the Plymouth United Savings Bank. From left to right are William Cassady (Roderick's father), telegraph operator; unidentified; Charles Chappell, express agent; Homer Singer, freight agent; Don Brown, baggage agent; Roderick Cassady; and Lester Chappell (Charles's father), by the baggage cart.

This view looks south toward the Starkweather Street railroad crossing in the 1940s. The Pere Marquette depot is on the south side of the tracks (at left), and the freight house is across the street from the depot (at right). In the 1970s, the freight house was moved to the north side of the tracks—on the east side of the street—to make way for a restaurant.

C&O Engine 107 is shown pulling into the station just past the Starkweather crossing. The small building on the left is the Railway Express Agency. Carts filled with packages are ready for transport. In the December 16, 1939, *Plymouth Mail*, Railway Express agent Leonard Millross encouraged readers to ship their packages "by railway express . . . You will be delighted with the convenience, the speed, and the economy of the service."

The activity at the depot diminished over the years as passenger service was discontinued. Hotel Victor (visible in the distance) survived for decades after the Sambrone brothers purchased it in 1905 and later renamed it Hotel Anderine. It was sold to Bob Gaddes in the 1960s. The name was changed to the Nelson Hotel and, subsequently, the Old Village Inn. On January 5, 1983, it was destroyed by fire and razed.

This is the freight house at its original location on the southwest side of the tracks at the Starkweather crossing. By February 1974, the building had been moved to the northeast side, making way for a new restaurant, the Golden Spike, which was to be housed in multiple renovated railcars; however, the project was never completed. The site remained vacant until 1981, when a new restaurant, Station 885, opened.

For many years, the freight house stood empty and unused. In late 1977, after extensive renovation, Saul and Adrienne Star brought the building back to life and opened the Village Freight House Gift Center. By 1983, Bob and Bonnie Beckinger were operating Plymouth Yard Hobbies and Gifts out of this building. At the time, it was one of only a few stores in the Detroit area that sold hobby trains.

This aerial photograph of the Starkweather Street crossing was taken in July 2018. Station 885 restaurant is visible at upper left. The old passenger depot appears at lower left, and the old freight house is at lower right. The long train coming around the bend has already stopped at least three cars that are waiting on southbound Starkweather Street. (Courtesy of and photograph by Peter Hayes.)

Eli Nowland worked as a teamster, or bus driver, for Harry Robinson's livery for 29 years. His duties included bringing passengers and express shipments to and from the railroad depot and mail to the post office. This 1914 view looks north up Oak Street (now Starkweather Street) from Blanche Street. Robinson's Livery was on today's Penniman Avenue. (Photograph by Davis Hillmer.)

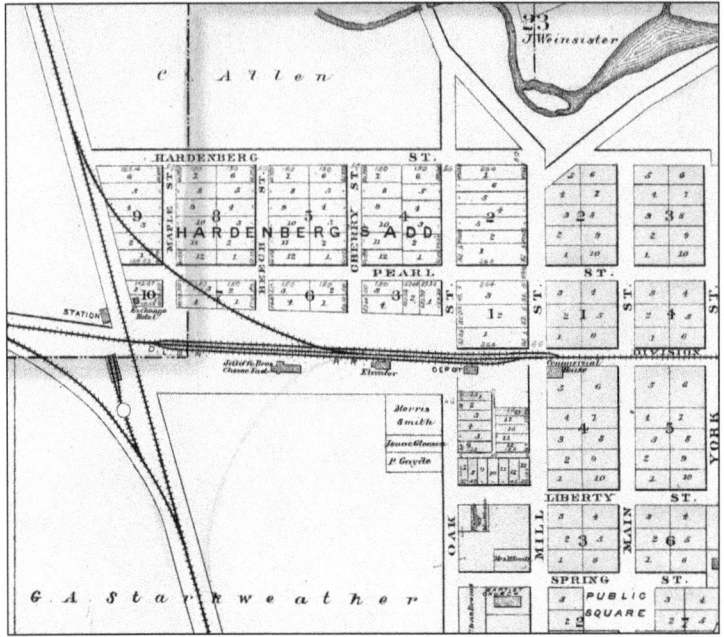

The *Detroit Free Press* reported in February 1893 that the Flint & Pere Marquette Railroad had recently completed a two-stall roundhouse at its junction with the Detroit, Lansing & Northern Railroad line in Plymouth. In the 1893 *Detailed Official Atlas of Wayne County, Michigan*, the roundhouse is shown in the southwest quadrant of the diamond with a track leading to a circle (turntable) and two tracks leading to a rectangle (roundhouse).

The first roundhouse burned to the ground in February 1910, according to the *Plymouth Mail*. It was soon replaced by an 8-stall roundhouse and 70-foot turntable (pictured). Additionally, the new roundhouse traded places with the old coal transfer house. The new coal transfer house used electricity, and the new turntable was operated by compressed air—both recent advances in train yard efficiency. (Courtesy of Clements Library.)

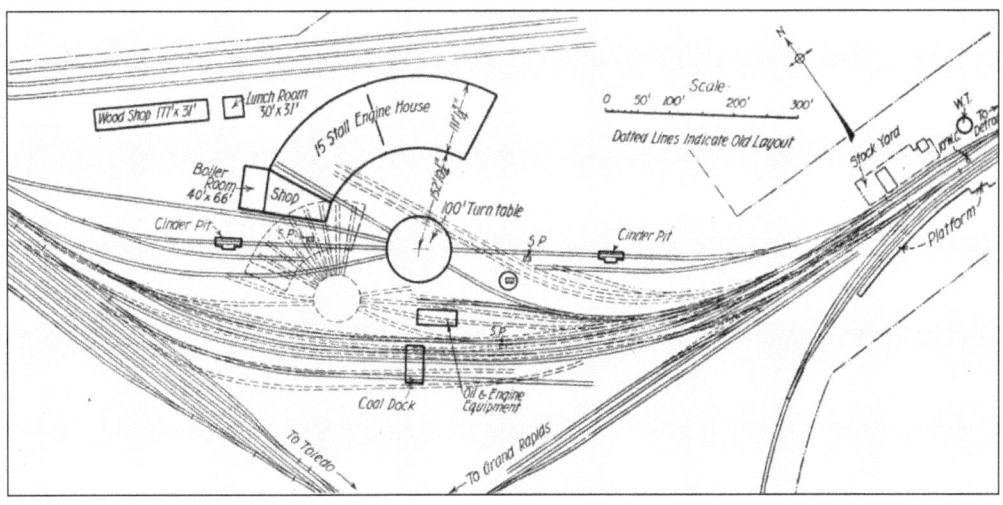

In June 1920, Pere Marquette announced it would spend $300,000 to improve the Plymouth yards. This drawing (above) shows many of the changes. The dotted lines represent the old layout, while the solid lines are the upgrades. In addition to a new 15-stall roundhouse and 100-foot turntable with a cemented pit floor, the company added a machine shop, a wood shop, a boiler room, and a lunchroom. The Arnold Construction Company of Chicago was the general contractor responsible for the construction as well as grading and lifting the tracks for the approach to the new facilities. The 15-stall Plymouth roundhouse was a majestic building, as shown in the 1925 view from the rooftop pictured below. The enhanced yard facilities allowed the workforce to grow, which contributed to the economy in Plymouth. (Above, courtesy of *Railway Review*; below, courtesy of Chesapeake & Ohio Historical Society.)

Steam locomotives were designed to run most efficiently in only one direction. Turntables were used to get the locomotives into specific stalls of the roundhouse, then to turn around those same locomotives once the repairs were done. Plymouth's 100-foot turntable (above) had a small cab next to the bridge where the pilot accessed all of the controls. Pere Marquette engine 393 (below), a 4-4-2, is shown rotating on the turntable around 1930. No. 393 was built by Brooks in 1901 and delivered to PM in 1902; it was scrapped in 1934. (Above, courtesy of Chesapeake & Ohio Historical Society.)

Philip (Harry) Norgrove came to Plymouth with his family in 1911 after a major forest fire destroyed the town of Au Sable, Michigan, where he had been working as a brickmason. He went to work in the Pere Marquette roundhouse. Here, he stands inside the brick roundhouse built in 1920–1921. All four of Harry's sons worked as engineers or firemen for the Pere Marquette. (Courtesy of Lynda Plotinski.)

In 1903, the Pere Marquette Railway Company spent $1,106 to purchase a wrecker for its fleet. The wrecker was used during the Salem train wreck in July 1907; the foreman of the wrecking train, Samuel Rummell, was killed in the train yard after returning from clearing the train wreck. In this photograph, Pere Marquette wrecker 52 is shown inside the Plymouth roundhouse in 1939. (Photograph by Cary Brace.)

This sweeping view of the Plymouth yard in about 1923 shows the recently completed roundhouse and turntable. One of two Robertson cinder pits, installed in 1919, is visible along the tracks. Farther down the track, near the turntable, is one of two standpipes used to deliver water to the locomotives. (Photograph by Charles Draper.)

The Great Depression hit the railroad industry hard. Many Plymouth yard workers were laid off for several years. Because of the downturn in traffic, sometime before 1936, Pere Marquette removed the turntable and eight of the roundhouse stalls. This February 1979 image shows the roundhouse still in use, with three tracks occupied by locomotives. The roundhouse closed in the 1980s and was torn down around 1992.

The Pere Marquette Railroad yard was a busy place in 1913. Freight trains on the left are having their cargo unloaded onto the freight house platform. Passenger cars sit idle on the right. The tall building in the distance is a water tower. The building above the passenger cars is a coal dock. This view looks west in the Plymouth Diamond, so named because of the intersection of the east–west and north–south lines.

Pere Marquette workers stand below the wood-framed coal dock in the Plymouth yard. This coal dock was built in 1910 on the grounds of the two-stall roundhouse that burned down. In 1916, it was replaced by a more modern and efficient coal dock that cost $25,000 to build.

At left is the Pere Marquette coal dock as it appeared in 1917, before the Plymouth yard went through major renovations following the end of World War I. Trains stopped their coal cars below the dock. Coal was delivered down a chute to the waiting coal car. This wooden coal dock burned in 1919 and was replaced the next year with a concrete coaling station. Below, in a 1940s image, engine 1229 darkens the sky as it heads out of Plymouth with freight bound for Grand Rapids. The PM's last coal dock in Plymouth looms over the train. The Pere Marquette's 40 Berkshire engines, built by Lima between 1937 and 1944, were the company's last steam-powered engines. (Below, courtesy of Kalmbach Media; photograph by Robert A. Hadley.)

This photograph shows the yardmaster's office in Plymouth; pictured are, from left to right, two unidentified men, Claude Robinson, and Ralph Hix. Robinson and Hix both graduated from Plymouth High School in 1910. The yardmaster's office started out as a tiny building. According to the Pere Marquette annual report of 1911, a new yard office was built to accommodate the increase in business that the yard was experiencing. (Courtesy of Clements Library; photograph by Roy Hinkley.)

The C&O communications microwave tower is prominently featured near the entrance to the Plymouth yard. Advancements in technology helped improve safety on the rails over the years but had a significant impact on the number of employees. In 1985, there were about 100 people working in this yard—about one-third of the workforce that was here in 1920. (Courtesy of Chesapeake & Ohio Historical Society; photograph by Gary House.)

Until November 2019, all that remained of the 15-stall roundhouse in the Plymouth yard were the foundation and the boiler room building that was connected to the roundhouse; the building is now gone. Train traffic through Plymouth has significantly decreased in the last decade, as CSX has pruned some of its lines because of a decline in business shipping. (Photograph by Marty Kerstens.)

This 2019 image of the Plymouth yard, taken by a drone positioned directly over the site of the former roundhouse, shows the boiler room building and semicircular foundation. It also shows the outlines of where the tracks were in each of the stalls. The big open area is where the turntable was located. (Photograph by Michael Shuster.)

Before automatic gates were installed, it was the watchman's duty to alert motorists of approaching trains. The watchman had a dangerous job. In September 1929, at the Main Street crossing pictured here, a car driven by Frederick Reiman Jr. hit watchman Joseph Robson; Reiman claimed that he did not see Robson standing in the middle of the street holding his lantern. The result was a broken leg for Robson.

This photograph, which looks north, offers a rare glimpse of the unblocked Sheldon Road crossing. The M-14 overpass, which opened in late 1979, is under construction in the background. Motorists were stopped at this crossing for long periods of time due to trains on multiple tracks, creating a potential hazard for emergency vehicles. The Sheldon Road CSX overpass project began in early 2007 to help alleviate issues at this crossing.

As part of the Sheldon Road overpass project, it was necessary for CSX to lay temporary tracks to the north of the new bridge location. The railroad workers couldn't wait for DTE Energy to remove a pole that was impeding their progress, so they laid the track anyway. In April 2008, the pole was removed, and the temporary tracks were put into service. (Courtesy of and photograph by Gene Dickirson.)

CSX trains began using the permanent tracks during the last week of October 2008, with about a dozen trains crossing per day. The temporary tracks were removed, allowing for excavation that was necessary in order to pave the road below the crossing. On December 12, Sheldon Road reopened after being closed for almost two years. The project cost over $15 million—nearly double the initial estimate. (Courtesy of and photograph by Gene Dickirson.)

Seven
Hobos, Presidents, and Circuses, Oh My!

The railroad afforded the opportunity for the transportation of freight and for ordinary visitors to travel to Plymouth. There were special visitors who arrived by rail, too. The presence of hobos in towns with rail stops was commonplace. One exceptional hobo was Harry D. Cooper, better known as "Railroad Jack," who defied the typical hobo stereotype with his dapper appearance and knowledge of history. The hobos who came through Plymouth would often set up camp in a place called Tramps Hollow, which was located in a wooded ravine just west of the village. Plymouth resident Herold Hamill remembered "going up there and seeing campfires and shelters in the brush." This legendary area was bulldozed when the M-14 freeway was put through in the late 1970s.

Throughout the years, Plymouth was a popular stop for politicians making their way across the state. In June 1900, the *Detroit Free Press* reported on Adm. George Dewey's stop in Plymouth on his way to Grand Rapids during the presidential campaign that year. Twelve years later, Theodore Roosevelt traveled to Plymouth, and in 1920, his son also made a visit. Pres. George H.W. Bush rounded out the list of visiting political leaders when he arrived in 1992.

The special visitors reaching Plymouth by rail were not just humans. Several unique trains also came through, including the Florida on Wheels exhibit in 1894, the Gentry Brothers Railroad Show in 1903, and the Ringling Bros. and Barnum & Bailey Circus in 1949. The community had multiple visits from the Artrain exhibit, bringing fine works of art by world-renowned masters for Plymouth citizens to enjoy. Additionally, when the steam train all but disappeared from regular service, it was a trip down memory lane when train enthusiasts once again heard the unique blast of the whistle when the 1914 Baldwin steamer, steam engine 1225, and the Chessie Steam Special No. 2101 graced the rails of Plymouth. All of these special visitors have played important roles in enhancing the history of the community and providing interesting entertainment, educational opportunities, and cultural enrichment.

On April 2, 1894, Plymouth experienced a part of the 1893 Chicago World's Fair when the Florida on Wheels train rolled into town. This marvel cost $20,000 to build and featured an exhibit that included live alligators. Before coming to Michigan, it had visited 20 other states and had "been seen by more people on earth than any other car," according to newspaper reports. (Courtesy of George A. Smathers Libraries, University of Florida.)

Tramps arriving by rail were frequently tired and hungry. They would often get arrested or surrender to the village marshal in order to get a free meal and temporary lodging, which cost about 50¢ per day in the 1880s and 1890s. This receipt for payment in 1887 is from Marshal Melville Weeks. It was rumored that Marshal Dan Smith arrested 38 hobos in one day in August 1897.

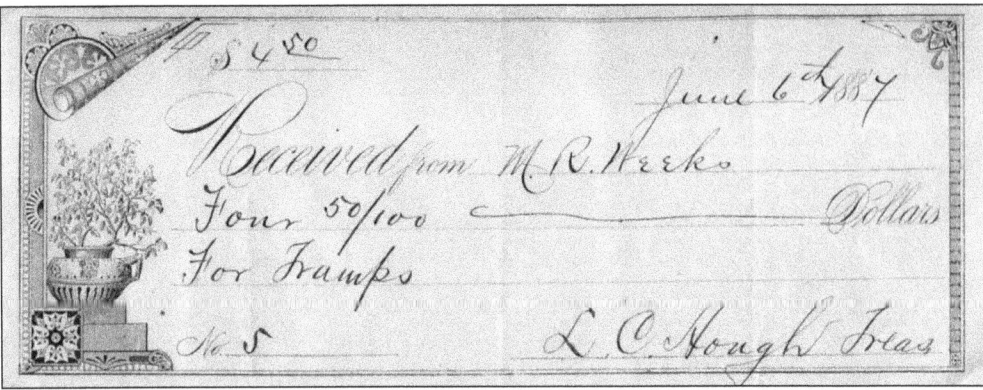

Harry D. Cooper, known as Railroad Jack, was considered a highbrow hobo. He attended Rush Medical College in Chicago before deciding to travel the rails in a hammock slung underneath a Pullman car. The cart that Cooper traveled with is pictured below. He had a passion for history and would challenge crowds to stump him on historical facts, offering $10 to anyone who could. Those who asked a question that he could answer would pay him a nickel; he amassed a great number of nickels and never paid out. As early as 1896, he was a regular visitor to Plymouth and soon became a legend. In 1931, he was the guest speaker at a Plymouth Kiwanis Club meeting. Two years later, he was found dead in an outbuilding of a gas station in Coldwater, Michigan. (Both, courtesy of Bentley Historical Library.)

At left, the Kaleidoscope Plymouth celebration was a series of events built around the Artrain's visit to Plymouth in 1972. The entire community was involved in this endeavor: schools, service groups, merchants, and local government officials. Helen Milliken, wife of Michigan governor William Milliken, was the general chair, with Jo Hulce of the Plymouth Community Arts Council spearheading the local effort. Gathered below for an on-site inspection of exhibit headquarters at the freight house near Starkweather Street are (left to right) city engineer Thomas Waffen; Murray Karsten, C&O divisional superintendent; William Henschell, general manager of the railroad's northern region; and Plymouth mayor James McKeon. (Below, photograph by Bob Woodring.)

The 1972 Artrain exhibit spent 18 days in Plymouth—its longest stop on the tour of the state. A walkway was created near the train and featured murals made by local students, as shown at right in the above photograph. This unique four-car art gallery (below) included a caboose and featured works of well-known artists such as Andrew Wyeth, Pablo Picasso, Andy Warhol, Henri Matisse, Auguste Renoir, Paul Cezanne, and Vincent van Gogh. The baggage car provided a place for the public to watch visiting artists at work as they demonstrated their crafts of sculpting, ceramics, graphics, and silversmithing. Artrain visited Plymouth again in 1987, for four days, and in 1989, when the exhibit theme was History of American Toys.

In celebration of the B&O Railroad's 150th birthday in 1977, the Chessie Steam Special 2101 went on tour. This locomotive was built in 1945 by the Reading Railroad and was designed for heavy freight and passenger service. It was retired from service in 1967 and was later saved from the scrapyard by Ross Rowland, founder of the American Freedom Train. After starting in Detroit, the June tour came through Plymouth to pick up passengers for daylong trips that passed through Lansing and Grand Ledge. A second and third tour in July traveled through Saginaw, Hoyt, and Clio. Adult passengers paid $20 for a regular coach ticket and up to $50 to travel in an observation or parlor car. The below photograph shows the Steam Special pulling out of Plymouth for the fourth tour as it headed to Grand Rapids. (Both, courtesy of and photograph by Bill Bresler.)

The visit of the Chessie Steam Special in 1977 was so overwhelmingly popular that it made an encore appearance the following year that coincided with the Old Village celebration of Dearie Days. The above photograph shows the train—filled with passengers—coming around the bend. The 2101, with its tender, was 110 feet and 6 inches in length, with the auxiliary tender adding 51 feet and 8¾ inches. The first tender carried 26 tons of coal and 19,000 gallons of water. The auxiliary tender carried an additional 16,000 gallons of water. The below photograph shows the burning embers being tended by the fireman. (Both, courtesy of and photograph by Bill Bresler.)

Former president Theodore Roosevelt arrived in Plymouth on Tuesday, October 8, 1912, as part of his tour promoting the Bull Moose Party. In anticipation of his arrival, school was dismissed, and the townspeople gathered at the station to welcome him. Just before the train pulled away, it backed up a few feet, and one little girl, Gladys Earl, was knocked down but sustained no injuries. The next day, the above photograph was taken at the station in Marquette, Michigan. Eight years later, on September 27, 1920, Roosevelt's son came through town en route to Flint. Theodore Roosevelt III (left) was introduced by Cass Benton on that rainy morning and spoke from the rear platform of the train to a large crowd of citizens from Plymouth and Northville. (Above, courtesy of Archives of Michigan; left, courtesy of Library of Congress.)

On September 26, 1992, Pres. George H.W. Bush and First Lady Barbara Bush arrived on the Spirit of America train during the 70-mile leg of their whistle-stop tour between Bowling Green and Plymouth. They were the first railroad passengers to disembark at this location in 20 years. (Courtesy of and photograph by Bill Bresler.)

President Bush delivered a 15-minute speech to an enthusiastic crowd of more than 12,000. This was the final destination on a two-day trip through Ohio and Michigan. Below, standing next to President Bush are, from left to right, Gov. John Engler; Michigan's first lady, Michelle Engler; and Michigan senator Robert Geake. Musical entertainment was provided by various groups, including the Plymouth Community Band and the Plymouth Fife and Drum Corps. The event concluded with a fireworks display.

Chesapeake & Ohio E7 No. 105 is pictured at left in the Plymouth roundhouse. In November 1954, the fifty millionth car produced by General Motors rolled off the assembly line in Flint, Michigan. The Chevrolet was painted gold and contained more than 600 gold-plated parts. This event was commemorated by C&O E7 No. 105 being painted gold with special lettering, as shown below on a regular run through Plymouth. This nod to General Motors was particularly significant considering the rail line in this area was a major hauler of automobiles and automobile components. (Both, courtesy of Chesapeake & Ohio Historical Society.)

The 1914 Baldwin steam locomotive chugged into town in June 1979 to replenish its 3,500-gallon water supply on the way to Greenfield Village. Trailing the engine were four cars: a Presidential Pullman car; a baggage car with original woodwork interior; a caboose; and a combination coach with parlor, baggage, and smoking compartments. After the cars reached Greenfield Village, they were put on permanent display. (Courtesy of and photograph by Bill Bresler.)

On Saturday, October 20, 1990, through the efforts of Project 1225 and the Michigan State Trust for Railway Preservation, steam engine 1225 hauled a freight train from Plymouth to Wyoming, Michigan. CSX Transportation arranged for this high-speed test in preparation for the 1225's excursion to the 1991 National Railroad Historical Society's convention in Huntington, West Virginia. This photograph was taken near Haggerty and Eckles Roads. (Courtesy of and photograph by Jeff Mast.)

This postcard is advertising the Gentry Brothers shows. The Gentry Brothers Railroad Show came to Plymouth in August 1903. The entire performance was given by marvelously trained ponies, dogs, monkeys, and elephants. One of the original steam calliopes that was part of the Gentry show is now part of the collection at the Henry Ford Museum in Dearborn, Michigan.

In July 1949, Ringling Bros. and Barnum & Bailey Circus trains came through Plymouth on their way from Flint. This photograph shows the rear cars and caboose of one of these lengthy trains. This circus traveled in four special trains that arrived at the Dearborn Pere Marquette siding, where they stayed during three days of performances in Detroit. (Courtesy of Chesapeake & Ohio Historical Society.)

Eight
LOCAL CONNECTIONS

Electric transit—also known as the interurban—came to Plymouth in 1898, when a franchise was given to the Detroit, Plymouth & Northville (DP&N) Railway Company. When it was fully functional in mid-1899, the line began on Michigan Avenue in Wayne and ran north to Cady's Corner (Wayne and Cherry Hill Roads), where it turned west; at Newburgh Road, the route turned north through Tonquish (a defunct village at Ford and Newburgh Roads) toward Newburg (now part of Livonia), where the route went northwest along Ann Arbor Street (now Ann Arbor Trail) into Plymouth. The tracks took a circuitous route through Plymouth, leaving the village along Northville Road. Going north, the line ran through the extinct village of Waterford and into the village of Northville for a distance of 14 miles. Passengers could transfer at Wayne to the Detroit, Ypsilanti & Ann Arbor Railway to go to Detroit. The opening of the line allowed visitors from other southeast Michigan locales to visit Plymouth and Northville within two hours.

In addition to passenger and freight cars, specialized cars could also be chartered for use along the rail lines. The funeral car, which was introduced in the area in 1902, was painted deep black with gold ornamentation. One portion of the car was used as a reception area for the placement of the casket; two wide doors on either side of the car led to this section. The other portion of the car could accommodate 34 passengers in plush upholstered seats. In September 1908, when Narcissa Garner of Northville died, a Detroit United Railway funeral car was used to transport her to Woodmere Cemetery in Detroit.

Safety along the lines was a constant concern. Accidents occurred frequently, which prompted the rail company to issue guidelines in an effort to help people avoid incidents. They advised signaling the motorman with lanterns, burning paper, or waving an arm. It was also suggested that one not cross in front of a moving car. By 1922, traveling by bus was less expensive, safer, and more efficient. Five years later, it was announced that interurban service between Wayne, Plymouth, Northville, and Farmington would be discontinued.

The merchants and citizens of Plymouth actively petitioned the village's common council to ensure the placement of DP&N rails down the middle of the streets of Plymouth. This petition, dated August 19, 1898, was signed by many prominent Plymouthites, including W.F. Markham, W.N. Wherry, Harry C. Robinson, L.H. Bennett, George Vandecar, O.H. Polley, J.G. Streng, C.A. Pinckney, and E.L. Riggs.

In July 1898, the route between Wayne and Plymouth was surveyed and staked out. Construction on the lines between the two villages began immediately. The first car to reach Plymouth on the new electric railway arrived on February 18, 1899. A large crowd was on hand to greet the car at the powerhouse on Ann Arbor Street (now Ann Arbor Trail), which was the end of the line. This view faces west on Ann Arbor Street.

When the winter weather cleared in April 1899, track was laid into and through the village of Plymouth. The above photograph shows construction of the lines on Ann Arbor Street from the Flint & Pere Marquette Railroad crossing and in front of the home (at right) that belonged to Melvin and Phoebe Patterson. A spur of track ran to the powerhouse behind the home. By June, cars were running to Main Street.

Once the tracks were laid, it was necessary to construct overhead lines to power the system. In May 1899, lines were installed throughout Plymouth. The expected date of completion was July 1. Citizens were disappointed when cars were still not running this route in time for the popular Plymouth Fair in September. After numerous delays, the first car reached Northville in November 1899. (Photograph by Charles Draper.)

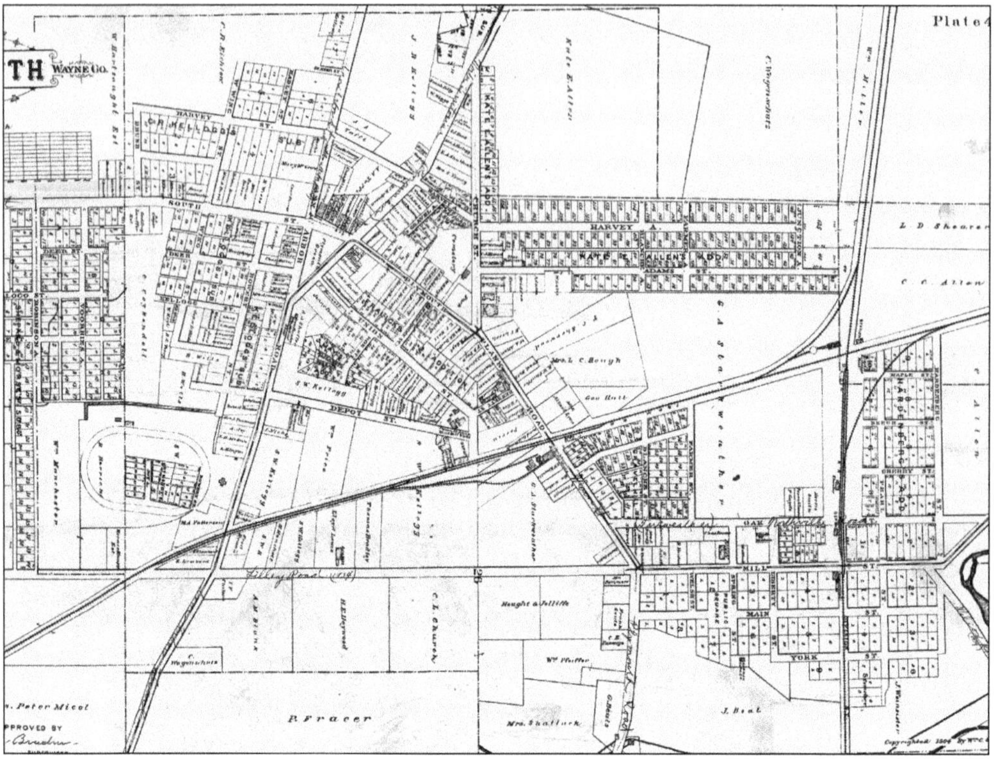

The interurban's circuitous route through Plymouth is shown above in a 1904 map. The track came in on Ann Arbor Street from the east, turned northwest on Sutton Street (now Penniman Avenue) along the north side of Kellogg Park, turned northeast on Main Street, crossed the Pere Marquette tracks again, turned north on Mill Street, then turned northwest to join with Oak/Starkweather Street where it turns into Northville Road. Below, a close-up of the map shows the intersection of the Pere Marquette Railroad tracks and the Detroit, Plymouth & Northville Railway lines. The Patterson house (pictured on page 89) is part of the property on the southwest corner of the intersection of the tracks. The powerhouse was also located here. The barn shown on page 88 belonged to Fred Reiman.

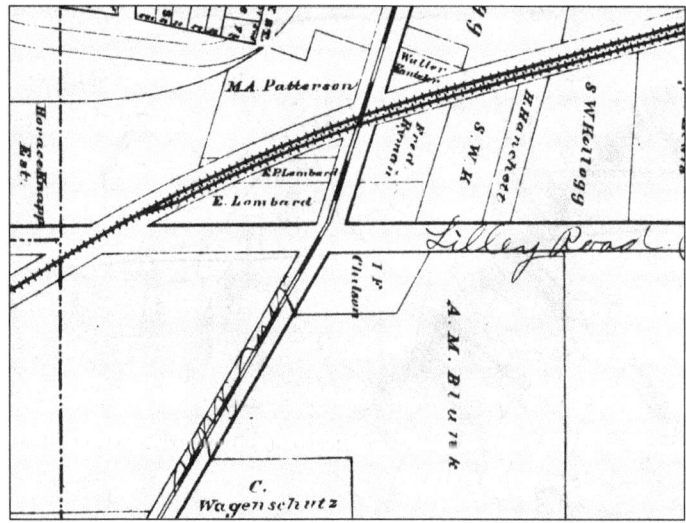

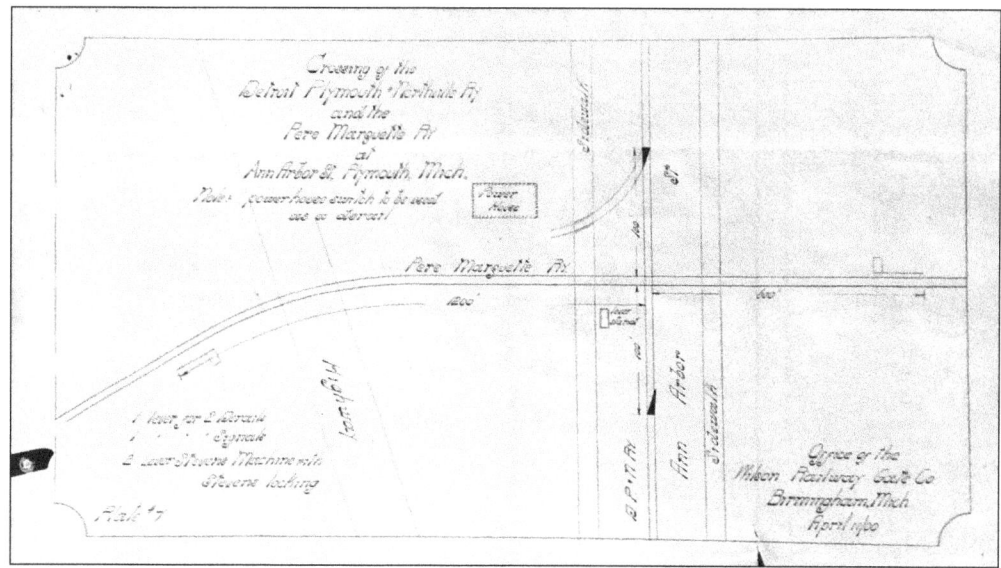

The April 1900 drawing above shows the addition of a new powerhouse switch at the junction of the railroad tracks and Ann Arbor Street. Plymouth resident Frank Henderson remembered that at the DP&N and F&PM crossings, the conductor had to get out, go to the tracks, and throw levers on the switches to warn trains. Once the interurban was across, the conductor had to take down the signal and catch up with the car. The DP&N depot in Wayne (pictured below) was built in 1898. It also served as a substation to boost DC power along the line. The automobile was still in its infancy, so electric rail provided the opportunity to easily travel to nearby communities. The depot served as both a passenger waiting room and a freight room. (Above, courtesy of Archives of Michigan, below, courtesy of Wayne Historical Museum.)

The Wayne depot, which fronted Michigan Avenue, had an addition built before 1914. This was the transfer point for travelers going north to Plymouth and Northville as well as those traveling east to Dearborn and Detroit and west to Jackson. By 1929, the popularity of automobiles rendered the electric railway obsolete, and the depot closed. It was demolished and replaced by a modern gas station in 1938. (Courtesy of Burton Historical Collection.)

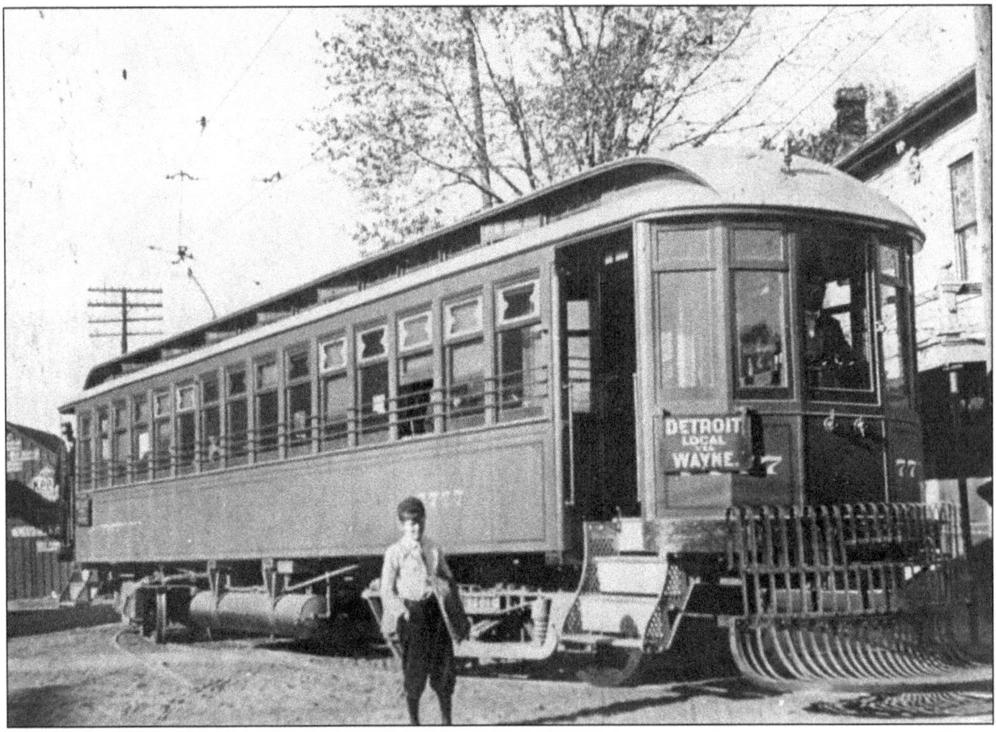

Newsboy Roger Cullen sold newspapers to electric rail passengers in Wayne. Note that car 7777 is labeled "Detroit Local via Wayne." Contemporary *Plymouth Mail* articles complained that passengers traveling from Detroit to Plymouth had difficulty finding the proper car to board because of the labeling. Cars on other routes listed all destinations. (Courtesy of Wayne Historical Museum.)

In December 1900, Plymouth merchants petitioned the village to allow the DP&N freight cars to stop near the corner of Main and Sutton Streets for delivery. Within a month, a combination waiting room and freight house was established north of Sutton Street on the east side of Main Street. In 1908, express freight service was established from Plymouth to Dearborn using the freight car shown here. (Courtesy of Burton Historical Collection.)

The Newburg depot was at the corner of Ann Arbor Street and Newburg Road. Plymouth resident Louise Spicer recalled the wedding trip of her parents, Sam and Alma Spicer. In December 1901, the Spicers waited here for more than an hour in the unheated waiting room in zero-degree temperatures for the car that took them to Wayne. They transferred to the Detroit, Jackson & Chicago car to spend their honeymoon in Marshall.

Central Park (now Kellogg Park) was more wooded in the early 20th century than it is today. In this photograph, an interurban car heads east on Sutton Street after turning off of Main Street. The first four cars of the Detroit, Plymouth & Northville Railway came from Pontiac. The cars had single Dupont trucks (wheel sets) and two General Electric 800 motors.

In this picture, an interurban car is approaching the Plymouth waiting room (at far left). Northbound cars stopped here every hour from 5:50 a.m. to 10:50 p.m. Southbound cars arrived 40 minutes past each hour. The cars also stopped at the Pere Marquette depot. The cars were popularly nicknamed "dinkies" from the inception of the DP&N until the Detroit United Railway (DUR) took over the line in 1908. (Photograph by Charles Draper.)

This view looks north at the intersection of Main and Sutton Streets. The Plymouth waiting room sign is protruding from the building in the distance at right. Conner Hardware is on the left. Popular conductor Charles Thumme was known to stop and buy eggs or would wait if someone who was usually at a certain spot was not there. (Photograph by Louis Pesha.)

The Yolande was an elegant parlor car used for private excursions around Detroit and outlying destinations along the electric rail lines. Here, the car is parked on the north side of Plymouth's Kellogg Park. Unlike typical passenger cars, the Yolande was carpeted, draped, lighted, heated, and furnished with tables, chairs, and a refrigerator. Guests were often treated to gourmet meals during these excursions. (Courtesy of Burton Historical Collection.)

Advance preparation was necessary in order to ensure clear passage for cars during the winter months. On October 2, 1908, the *Plymouth Mail* reported: "The management of the railway is already preparing for winter. The plans include the equipment of two construction cars with the latest device to sweep the snow far from the rails on either side, sections of snow fences along the interurban lines where there is greatest danger of drifts and snow scrapers to be put on many of the cars." The above photograph shows freshly fallen snow being cleared from the tracks on Main Street heading into Plymouth. The car in the below photograph is traveling on the clean track as it passes by the site where the Plymouth Historical Museum now stands.

In this image looking south from the corner of Church and Main Streets around 1923, the rail tracks are visible in the middle of the brick-paved road. The sharing of the roadway presented a challenge for motorists, pedestrians, and conductors. Accidents were common—and sometimes fatal. The railroad commission put regulations in place, like requiring streetcars to stop at the nearest street corner, to help prevent mishaps. (Photograph by Charles Draper.)

A car is visible in the distance in this picture of a tree-lined Mill Street. On this street, near Carl Heide's greenhouse, John Reece of Detroit needed assistance boarding the car in May 1917. He was inside the door when the car started to move. Being unsteady on his feet, he fell from the car and onto the ground. Luckily, he only suffered a minor injury to his shoulder. (Photograph by Davis Hillmer.)

The interurban tracks on Mill Street are visible here, while a car in the far distance is rounding the turn at Main Street. At right is the home of John Christian Peterhans, a Civil War veteran and well-respected brickmason who played an important role in building the Daisy factory. The Baptist church next to the house was the site where Carry Nation, a radical member of the temperance movement, lectured on September 13, 1908.

The trestle passing over the Rouge River could accommodate horse-and-buggy traffic as well as railway cars. This car is headed for Northville with six passengers. The motorman and conductor are in uniform at the ends of the coach. Candler Brothers of Detroit built this bridge and two others between Plymouth and Northville in May 1899.

On March 12, 1920, the dam at Phoenix Mill burst as a result of overwhelming ice and water flow. The interurban track, located above the dam, was compromised and deemed impassable, as shown here. The *Plymouth Mail* reported: "Fred Beyer, who is the engineer at the Pere Marquette pump house on the River Rouge, had a narrow escape from drowning . . . with the breaking of the dam on the river above. . . . It was only by clinging to a wire fence that he was able to reach higher land and safety." This was not the first time that the dam had given way. Similar incidents had occurred in February 1900 and March 1904. It was a challenge for section crews to repair the tracks, and on one occasion, it was almost two weeks before cars were running again.

In this postcard that looks north along the road from Plymouth to Northville, a car is near the icehouse that was purchased by J.C. Hartz sometime after 1899. Phoenix Mill, which produced Plymouth Wheat Flakes, was located here until it burned down in July 1905. There was an ongoing property dispute between the DUR and Hartz. By 1909, the DUR was paying Hartz $100 per month for the use of the land.

By 1922, the iron bridge shown in the photograph at the top of this page was replaced with one made of concrete. The driveway approaches for the new plant built by Henry Ford on the former site of Phoenix Mill are visible on the left. As roadways continued to improve, automobile travel gained popularity and had a negative impact on the number of passengers choosing to travel by interurban. (Photograph by Charles Draper.)

In late 1899, passengers of the interurban traveling from Plymouth to Northville were inconvenienced by having to make a transfer at Phoenix Mill, as the existing tracks used by the Flint & Pere Marquette Railroad were in the way of direct passage. In October 1899, the state crossing board mandated that the interurban had to tunnel under the tracks of the Flint & Pere Marquette to provide a more efficient route.

As they traveled along Northville Road, the interurban tracks passed through 10 acres of property owned by the Benton family. Car 7767 is shown in this photograph near what is now Cass Benton Park, known for its rolling hills and towering trees. Benton, along with Edward Hines and Henry Ford, was instrumental in creating the Wayne County Road Commission. (Courtesy of the Burton Historical Collection.)

Laying the tracks for the interurban was not an easy task. This photograph shows a crew of four men using a team of horses to plow a trough down the middle of Main Street in Northville in front of Stark Brothers' shoe store. The tracks ran from Main Street to Northville Road on the way to Plymouth. (Courtesy of Northville Historical Society.)

The rail crew, often called gandy dancers, are shown here at the Northville freight depot on their hand-pump section car. These hardworking men used picks, shovels, ballast forks, and lining bars to maintain the track. William White (second from left) worked for the Detroit United Railway for 33 years. He served as the superintendent in charge of the tracks between Farmington and Plymouth. (Courtesy of Northville Historical Society.)

The Northville express office and freight depot were located on the northeast corner of Griswold and Main Streets. Milk and produce from nearby farms were shipped throughout the region from this location. Parmenter's Cider Mill used the DUR system to send barrels of apple cider to its customers. It took about 15 minutes to get from Northville to Plymouth by dinky, which was less time than it would take for a five-gallon wooden tub of ice cream to melt on its way from Ambler House Confectionery in Northville to Murray's Ice Cream Store in Plymouth. (Both, courtesy of Northville Historical Society.)

In March 1899, Frank Bell sold interurban tickets at his store on Sutton Street in Plymouth. That year, the 5¢ ticket granted passage from Northville to Plymouth. By 1918, rates had increased to 6¢, with a 1¢ charge for transfers. This increase was protested by Cass Benton, which resulted in the company agreeing to keep the 5¢ rate for travel between Waterford and either Northville or Plymouth. (Courtesy of Northville Historical Society.)

This time schedule from 1910 shows the range of opportunity for passengers to travel from Detroit to Jackson and numerous points between. In 1922, bus service was gaining in popularity, with advertised fares costing less than what was being charged for the interurban. By February 1927, it was announced that interurban service between Wayne, Plymouth, Northville, and Farmington would be discontinued. (Courtesy of Wayne Historical Museum.)

Nine

The End of the Train

The most generally accepted story of the origin of the car called a caboose dates back to the early 1800s, when conductor Nat Williams, on the Auburn & Syracuse Railroad, desired a more comfortable space to do his paperwork. Williams is credited with repurposing an unused boxcar at the end of the train to create a remote office. This afforded him the space he needed and allowed for the storage of necessary items like lanterns, flags, and spare parts. Over the years, what was first referred to as the "conductor's car" caught on across the industry.

Modifications to this specialized car—such as cupolas, bay windows, porches, and ladders—helped increase safety on the rails. The advent of the cupola took place when a hole was placed in a boxcar roof to help the crew get a better view of the train. Additions like a stove, a toilet, and bunks also provided added comfort for the crew. The iconic railroad caboose, made of wood and usually painted red for increased visibility, was a staple on the end of every freight train in the late 19th century. By the early 20th century, cabooses were being fabricated from steel. The 1980s brought new labor agreements that reduced the hours of service for train crews. The caboose, no longer needed to house a crew overnight, quickly became obsolete.

CO 904151, built in 1980, was among the last group of cabooses manufactured in North America. It served in the Wyoming Yard in Grand Rapids, Michigan, was taken out of service in the late 2000s, and sat, waiting to be scrapped. In 2015, however, it was removed from storage tracks and taken to the car shop to be refurbished so it could be used for a yard job. Later that year, CO 904151 was being prepped for a new paint scheme when the project was suddenly canceled. The caboose was still in use until early 2019, when it was shipped to Rougemere Yard in Dearborn, Michigan, awaiting delivery to its new permanent home at the Plymouth Historical Museum.

Caboose CO 904151 was built in July 1980 by Fruit Growers Express of Alexandria, Virginia, as part of a 160-car order. The cars from this order were split between the Baltimore & Ohio and the Chesapeake & Ohio. By 1983, when this photograph was taken, nine of the cabs from this order were located in Plymouth. Caboose CO 904151 was stationed in Grand Rapids, Michigan. (Courtesy of and photograph by Dwight Jones.)

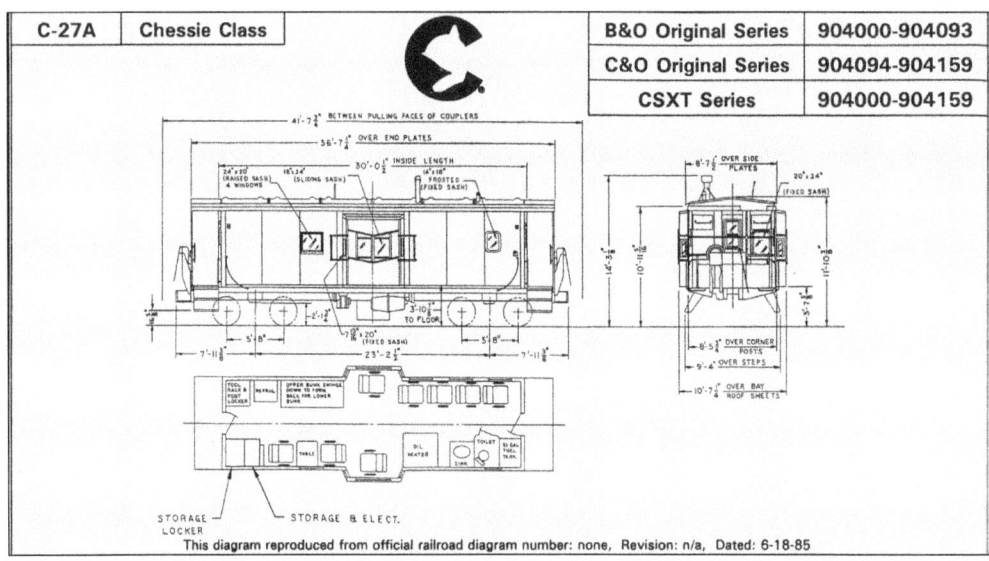

The Class C27-A cabooses were built of steel and replaced the diminishing number of wood-sheathed cabs that remained in service into the 1970s. This thoroughly modern bay-window design was standard for B&O and did not incorporate the cupola that was commonplace on C&O models. These were some of the last cabooses built for use in North America. (Courtesy of CSX.)

In the 1980s, cabooses were eliminated from most trains. Technology upgrades, such as line defect detectors and end-of-train devices, provided improvements in monitoring and safety and resulted in a reduction of the number of necessary crew members. As the need diminished for the caboose to house multiple crew members, cabooses were repurposed for use as shoving platforms. This type of car is used when a train is engaged in a reverse move. In both of these photographs taken at the Wyoming Yard in Grand Rapids, caboose CO 904151 is being used as a shoving platform to provide a safe place for the foreman or switchman to stand. (Both, courtesy of and photograph by Jonathon Leese.)

In both of these photographs, a switchman stands safely on the platform of caboose CO 904151 awaiting the movement of a train in the Wyoming Yard. In the 1980s, most of the freight traffic going through this yard was related to the automotive, agriculture, and coal industries. More than 25 trains per day were passing through at that time. This yard also served as an important maintenance base for the Chessie System where most Chessie cabooses were repaired, rebuilt, or serviced. It was not uncommon for more than 50 cabooses to be waiting to be cycled through the car shop at one time. (Both, courtesy of and photograph by Jonathon Leese.)

Caboose CO 904151 was retired in the late 2000s. It was briefly put back into service in 2015 and fitted with new trucks and wheels and refurbished brake rigging. It was one of only two usable cabooses in West Michigan. In early 2019, it was sent to CSX's Rougemere Yard in Dearborn, where it awaited transfer to its new home in Plymouth. (Courtesy of CSX.)

A project of this magnitude includes a lot of moving parts and cooperation from many different entities. Reliable Landscaping began preparing the subgrade for the railroad track in May 2019. After the area was cleared, a bottom layer of railroad ballast was put in place. The ballast was donated by Ontario Trap Rock. The railroad ties were donated by CSX. (Photograph by Elizabeth Kelley Kerstens.)

Alfonsi Railroad Construction was hired to build the railroad using traditional construction techniques. At left, workers attach tie plates to railroad ties using spikes donated by CSX. Two 40-foot pieces of steel rail (shown below) were privately donated. The rails are date-stamped 1945 and were made in Illinois. The rails had to be cut in half in order to be transported. Workers needed to reconnect the rails with joint bars before putting them in place on the tie plates. The joint bars are held in place with six bolts—a standard for jointed rail segments in the United States. (Both, photograph by Elizabeth Kelley Kerstens.)

Once the rails were reconnected, they were placed on the tie plates, as shown at right. Precise measurements were used to ensure the railroad ties lined up correctly. A hydraulic jack was used to pound the rail spikes into place. The same process was used to install the second rail. This method of railroad construction has been used for many years, although it is more common for new railroads to be built using automation and machinery. After Alfonsi Railroad Construction completed work, Reliable Landscaping returned to fill in the remainder of the railroad ballast, as shown below. The Plymouth Historical Museum's railroad was now complete and ready for the arrival of caboose CO 904151. (Both, photograph by Elizabeth Kelley Kerstens.)

Delivering the caboose—using a custom tractor trailer and public roads—was a complicated endeavor. Marc Kalis has moved almost three dozen train cars over the years and has perfected the process. The first step (above) involved bringing one set of trucks (train wheels, suspension, and brakes) to the installation site. The trucks were moved off the flatbed with temporary rails and a pulley system. Kalis (center) and his wife, Sharon (left), accomplished the transfer, while Marty Kerstens (right) ensured the trucks didn't roll too far down the track. At long last, in mid-June 2019, the caboose rolled down Main Street (below) on its custom carrier driven by Kalis. That's not a sight one sees every day. (Both, photograph by Elizabeth Kelley Kerstens.)

Positioning the caboose so that it was in line with the track was tricky in the tight area between the museum and Plymouth City Hall. Kalis backed up the tractor trailer as close as possible to the track. Note the custom trailer attached to the rig in the above photograph. In order to transport the caboose, the front steps on both sides and both train trucks had to be removed from it. The caboose was carried on top of two sets of temporary wheels. The next step (below) was removing one set of temporary wheels in preparation for reuniting the truck with the caboose on the track. Hydraulic lifts were placed on both sides of the caboose to elevate it high enough so that the temporary wheels could be removed. (Both, photograph by Elizabeth Kelley Kerstens.)

Temporary rail had to be positioned just right, aligning both sets of rails. The truck already on the track was pushed underneath the caboose, lining up the center plates. The center plate on the caboose fit in the center plate on the truck, which allowed the truck to turn freely underneath it. The caboose was then hydraulically lowered onto the truck. (Photograph by Elizabeth Kelley Kerstens.)

Once the caboose and truck were reunited, Marc Kalis used his rig to push the caboose along the track. Kalis's son Danny watched as the caboose moved down the track, constantly communicating with his father to ensure the move went as planned. Note that there is no door on the caboose—one of the surprises encountered upon delivery of the caboose. (Photograph by Elizabeth Kelley Kerstens.)

The hydraulic lifts were used once again to prop up the end of the caboose in order to remove the second set of temporary wheels. Here, Marc Kalis ensures proper placement of the hydraulic lift. With the caboose weighing 67,500 pounds, any mistakes could be costly. (Courtesy of and photograph by Bill Bresler.)

With the caboose propped up on the hydraulic lifts, the second set of temporary wheels could be removed, and the caboose was ready to receive its other truck. For insurance and liability purposes, plywood doors were crafted and attached in order to keep the curious out of the caboose. (Photograph by Elizabeth Kelley Kerstens.)

Above, temporary rails were again put in place to move the second truck off the flatbed and under the caboose. The temporary track was kept together with steel bars bolted into place to ensure the track could withstand the weight of the truck. The truck was slowly lowered into place through the use of a pulley system. Below, Danny Kalis is operating the hydraulic lift; he had to raise the caboose higher to ensure the truck could navigate the angle of the track without hitting the undercarriage of the caboose. (Above, photograph by Elizabeth Kelley Kerstens; below, courtesy of and photograph by Bill Bresler.)

Above, Marc Kalis watches over the truck and the track, always mindful that the slightest mistake could make it difficult to maneuver the truck. The entire moving team consisted of only three men. At right, coauthor Elizabeth Kerstens celebrates as caboose CO 904151 is pulled into place on its final ride. Kerstens is the executive director of the Plymouth Historical Museum and oversaw the caboose project, including negotiations with CSX and the City of Plymouth and arranging for landscaping, track building, caboose moving, and caboose renovations. (Above, photograph by Elizabeth Kelley Kerstens; right, courtesy of and photograph by Bill Bresler.)

Above, after much anticipation and anxiety, the museum's caboose was finally in place and awaiting restoration. Despite outward appearances and being minus two doors, the caboose arrived in generally good shape. CSX quickly began a search for replacement doors. In August 2019, Rick Westphal, from CSX in Toledo, drove to the Wyoming Yard in Grand Rapids and removed two doors from a sister caboose there. Westphal (left) delivered the doors the next day with the assistance of the Plymouth Historical Museum's facility manager, Mike Hoggard. The doors were in rough shape, with the glass broken on one of the windows and the hinges needing repairs. (Above, photograph by Mike Woloszyk; left, photograph by Elizabeth Kelley Kerstens.)

In addition to donating the caboose, in 2014 CSX generously donated a working crossbuck to the museum. For five years, it was located outside the museum's Church Street door, with its lights flashing and bell ringing when the museum was open. In mid-August 2019, Marc Kalis returned with his forklift to move the crossbuck close to the caboose. The stabilizing section of the tall crossbuck extended four feet below the surface, so a corresponding hole had to be dug deep and wide enough to allow for leveling. With the help of his forklift, Kalis was able to deftly remove the crossbuck from its original location. The journey down the sidewalk was slow, as Kalis took care to make sure the lanky sign remained upright and stable. Once the crossbuck was lowered into place, it was secured to the caboose until workers could backfill the hole to make the sign stable. Soon after, an electrician reattached the lights, which once again flash when the museum is open. The bell was not hooked up again. (Photograph by Elizabeth Kelley Kerstens.)

Restoration of the caboose's exterior began in late August 2019 under the direction of contractor T.J. Gaffney of Streamline Historic Services, LLC. Gaffney hired experienced and talented painter Jeff Conner of Railcar & Military Equipment Painting in Pennsylvania. The first step (above) was washing the caboose and masking the windows and other areas not receiving paint. Work began on the roof, which received two coats of silver paint. Conner and his two assistants painted the underframe and the trucks (wheels) black, as shown below. The original specifications called for the underframe and trucks to be "enchantment blue." Gaffney chose black because these items were typically repainted black on the caboose's first trip to a paint shop. (Both, photograph by Elizabeth Kelley Kerstens.)

After the underframe and trucks were repainted, two coats of primer were applied to the rest of the areas that had not yet been painted. The caboose was ready to return to its original "signal yellow" color. The transformation of CO 904151 from a rust-laden and pockmarked train car to a beautiful, bright yellow caboose with its original 1980s look was well underway. Remarkably, this caboose still had its original paint scheme and stencils. Since the caboose had not been repainted during its entire 39 years of service, Jeff Conner was able to easily replicate all of the stenciling, as shown below. To reapply the bigger stencils, Conner used a combination of freehand and tracing with graphite. (Both, photograph by Elizabeth Kelley Kerstens.)

The doors (left) were painted separately to avoid any overspray. After the windows and other parts were masked, the enchantment blue paint was applied to the doors. This color was also originally on the underframe and trucks, but those are painted black on this caboose. Below, all of the lettering and symbols on the yellow background were painted in enchantment blue. Jeff Conner deftly hand-painted the larger numbers and symbols, including the Chessie the Cat mascot incorporated into the big "C" for the Chesapeake & Ohio Railway. Chessie was first introduced in an ad in *Fortune* magazine in 1933. The logo was so popular that C&O incorporated it into its marketing materials for years. (Both, photograph by Elizabeth Kelley Kerstens.)

Master painter Jeff Conner is shown standing on a ladder on one end of the caboose. His paper stencil of the car number was positioned so he could trace the numbers with graphite. Once that process was completed, he hand-painted the caboose number—904151—with enchantment blue. He did this on both ends of the caboose. (Photograph by Elizabeth Kelley Kerstens.)

Here, Jeff Conner puts the finishing touches on the safety cross logo that appeared on C&O cabooses made in 1980. That year, C&O had a major campaign underway to spread the word about safety at railroad crossings. The campaign lasted for 14 months and was considered a success as far as reducing railroad-crossing accidents. (Courtesy of and photograph by T.J. Gaffney.)

After the exterior was updated, the upgrade of the caboose interior was next on the docket. In the image at left, the interior shows gentle wear on the wood flooring and upholstery despite being almost 40 years old. Some of the wood flooring underneath the bay windows will be replaced. The sleeping berths are visible on the right side; the top bunk could be folded down to form a back for the lower bunk in order to use this compact space most efficiently. The oil heater and sink are on the left. The photograph below shows the area beyond the bunks, with the refrigerator, a tool rack, and a footlocker. A table and reversible chairs allowed the crew to keep up with paperwork like that in the wall racks. The bay windows are intact, with their original diagonally sliding screens and windshield wipers on the small side windows. (Both, photograph by Marty Kerstens.)

The exterior restoration was completed over Labor Day weekend in 2019. Above, the small-lettered stencils have been completed. These were created by a local company and hand-painted by Jeff Conner's team. The lettering on the blue trim above the trucks is yellow. There are also vermilion orange stripes along the top and bottom of the caboose. With the exterior work completed, landscaping work continued. Reliable Landscaping returned and installed the brick paver sidewalk shown along the left side of the caboose in the below photograph. Engraved pavers are for sale as a fundraiser to support the caboose restoration. (Both, photograph by Elizabeth Kelley Kerstens.)

Bibliography

Community Crier, 1963–2002.
Detroit Free Press, 1867–2010.
Detroit, Lansing & Northern Railroad Annual Reports, 1877–1894.
Dickirson, Gene D. *The Sheldon Road Project*. Plymouth, MI: GDT Speedster, 2009.
Dixon, Thomas W., Jr. *C&O for Progress: The Chesapeake & Ohio at Mid-Century*. Clifton Forge, VA: Chesapeake & Ohio Historical Society, 2008.
———. *Chesapeake & Ohio's Pere Marquettes*. Lynchburg and Clifton Forge, VA: TLC Publishing and the Chesapeake & Ohio Historical Society, 2004.
Flint & Pere Marquette Railroad Annual Reports, 1870–1898.
Jones, Dwight. *Steel Cabooses of the Chesapeake & Ohio, 1937–1987*. Parsons, WV: McClain Printing Company, 1987.
Michigan Gazetteers, 1863–1922.
Million, Arthur B., and Thomas W. Dixon Jr. *Pere Marquette Power*. Clifton Forge, VA: Chesapeake & Ohio Historical Society, 1984.
Northville Record, 1869–2000.
Plymouth Historical Museum Archive.
Plymouth Mail/Observer, 1887–2000.
Vander Yacht, Clifford J. *The Pere Marquette in 1945*. Clifton Forge, VA: Chesapeake & Ohio Historical Society, 2008.

About the Friends of the Plymouth Historical Museum

The Friends of the Plymouth Historical Museum is a privately funded membership organization dedicated to preserving, teaching, and presenting history through the operation and support of the Plymouth Historical Museum. The Friends (also known as the Plymouth Historical Society) was organized in 1948 with 52 original members. It owns and operates the Plymouth Historical Museum. The museum originally opened in 1962 in an historic home. By 1971, the museum had outgrown its space. A new, purpose-built museum building opened its doors to the public on February 14, 1976; an addition was completed in 2001. The museum is housed in a beautiful, 26,000-square-foot building donated by Margaret Dunning in memory of her parents, Charles and Bessie Dunning. The Plymouth Historical Museum is located at 155 South Main Street in Plymouth. It features a late-19th-century Victorian re-creation of Main Street that traces the growth of the small town from the railroad depot to the general store. The largest Abraham Lincoln collection on exhibit in the state of Michigan is housed in a separate room off of Main Street. A timeline of Plymouth in the lower level features displays of Ford Village Industries, the Alter Motor Car, World War II, communication history, and Plymouth's air rifle industry. The museum hosts three special exhibits each year to highlight the depth of the collections and showcase Plymouth as a microcosm of small-town America. In 2019, the Plymouth Historical Museum received a gift of a caboose donated by CSX Corporation. The caboose allows the museum to further interpret Plymouth's rich railroad history within a unique and historic setting.

For more information on the Plymouth Historical Museum, visit www.plymouthhistory.org or call 734-455-8940.

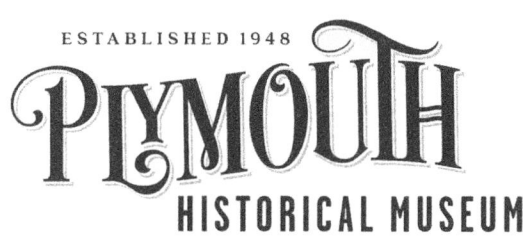

Visit us at
arcadiapublishing.com

www.ingramcontent.com/pod-product-compliance
Lightning Source LLC
Chambersburg PA
CBHW060938170426
43194CB00027B/2987